First published in 2009 by
Liberties Press
Guinness Enterprise Centre | Taylor's Lane | Dublin 8
Tel: +353 (1) 415 1224
www.LibertiesPress.com | info@libertiespress.com

Distributed in the United States by
Dufour Editions | PO Box 7 | Chester Springs | Pennsylvania 19425

and in Australia by
InBooks | 3 Narabang Way | Belrose NSW 2085

Trade enquiries to CMD Distribution
55A Spruce Avenue | Stillorgan Industrial Park
Blackrock | County Dublin
Tel: +353 (1) 294 2560 | Fax: +353 (1) 294 2564

Copyright © Donna Kennedy, 2009

The author has asserted her moral rights.

ISBN: 978–1–905483–61–7
2 4 6 8 10 9 7 5 3 1

A CIP record for this title is available from the British Library.

Cover design by Ros Murphy
Internal design by Liberties Press
Printed in Ireland by Colour Books | 105 Baldoyle Industrial Estate | Dublin 13

Step On, Step Up

The Irish Guide to Buying Your First Home
and Moving Up the Property Ladder

Donna Kennedy

LIB
ERT
IES

To those who bring happiness into people's lives

Contents

Introduction

What if I was to tell you that in just a few months' time you will own your own property? There'll be no more worrying about where you're going to live next and you won't have to ask permission to do every little thing. Wouldn't it be fantastic to wake up in the morning and know that your money works for you, not you for it? That's just dreamer-talk, though, isn't it? How could one possibly expect to get on the property ladder in today's market? Well I'm here to tell you that you absolutely can, *especially* in today's market!

I'm sure that might be hard for you to swallow at first, given all the hype about the current state of the property market. Over the last while, we've all been subjected to that evil-eyed monster called *recession*. Splashed in the papers, peering out from our TV screens – it's everywhere. But the truth is, that monster has always been there and always will be there. It's nothing new. If we look back through history, it's showed its face several times. Look at the 1980s – an absolute disaster! People panicked and even left the country. But not the smart guys! The smart guys hung around. They saw opportunity! Big opportunity.

The fact is, and they will tell you, it's not the state of the market that predicts suffering. It's how you view the market and how you play it that determines your success. History shows, time and time again, that property can be bought in any market, in any country, at any time. With the right information, the right strategies and the right attitude, you can get on the property ladder even in the shabbiest of markets. And what's more, when you're on the ladder, you can climb it. Do you honestly think property tycoons wait around for economists to give them the go-ahead? Of course they don't. They acknowledge situations but they don't get stuck in them. They draw on the intelligence of those who've come before them and they take positive action. So you can either be ruled by fear and ultimately stay where you are, or you can use that lovely brain of yours and get results. *Now* is the time to do it!

You have the right mindset to do this. You picked up this book when you could easily have left it on the shelf. That tells me that something inside you told you that you're not going to settle for second best anymore. You're willing to step up and take action. You're willing to learn.

I know it probably seems impossible for you to get on the property ladder right now, and if you're anything like I was, the concept might even scare you. I was also bombarded by all the horror stories when I bought my first place. I know what it's like to have people tell you you're better off to play it safe and rent. The old 'what if it all goes wrong' jazz. But after shelling out over €36,000 in just three years, I couldn't do the renting scene anymore. To me, it was dead money. OK, I had a place to live, and I guess that was something, but when all was said and done I knew I could be turfed out at a moment's notice and have nothing. At least if you're paying a mortgage you have something to show for it.

The problem for me was that I didn't know anything about property starting out. It felt like being dumped alone in a foreign country and not understanding the language. All the books I read were full of technical gobbledegook. All the people I spoke to made property buying sound so intimidating. And what's more, debt scared the hell out of me. Basically, I was a lost cause who wanted something badly but didn't know how to get it. I feared the unknown and I feared messing up. And with self-doubt visiting me on a regular basis, I bottled it and continued to rent.

But about three months later, a couple of friends and I went abroad for a few days. One of them happened to be into property, and on the last day of the holiday he wanted to check out a new development he'd heard about. I went with him. Next thing I knew, I was back in Ireland – each of us handing over a deposit for an apartment! It suddenly dawned on me: I'd gone barking mad. I was buying an apartment with no clue what I was doing. As luck would have it, I decided to bite the bullet and follow through with it. I figured that I would just copy every move my friend made. And I did.

In hindsight, although the apartment was a solid investment and I still own it today, it would have made more sense to secure my own house first. I wasted money on rent that I could have used on home mortgage payments. So for our purposes here, we're going to get you your own house first, and then if you want you can go on and buy more. In your hands, you have a straight-forward guide to getting you an outstanding result. You're going to own your own place very soon, so let's get excited and let's get started!

1

Where and What

Prepare to buy before you buy. Don't buy anything, any-where. Buy smart.

You've heard the phrase 'location, location, location', and it's not rocket science to know that it needs to be considered when you're buying property. But you're going to think about that phrase, and pretty much everything else, in a whole new way here. It's common knowledge that it's better to buy the worst property in the best location (with a view to doing it up) than it is to buy the best house in the worst location. But how many first-time buyers could even afford that worst house? Even if they were to get it at a rock-bottom price (you'll learn how to do that), it would probably still be outside the range of a first-time-buyer budget. So people tend to either buy whatever they can, wherever they can, and pay the going price, or buy nothing at all. If they do buy, they buy the obvious. But obvious is not necessarily smart.

Put in a little preparation now, look outside the box and reap rewards.

The Big Question

This is the question you need to ask yourself: is it a given that the location in vogue now will always be the location in vogue? Is it possible that another location could be in vogue in the future?

Of course it is! You just need to know how to spot that location before anyone else gets their paws on it. You've got to spot the diamond in the rough. And you're very unlikely to find that in the obvious.

Let's say that you want the city lifestyle but your budget won't allow for it. The obvious thing would be to buy as close to the city as possible, right? Well, that's a no-brainer. Buying in or close to a city is always likely to be a good investment. But if you want more than just a good investment, there's a bit more to it. To get a great investment, it's not just about buying in or close to where it's all happening, it needs to be in the area where *it's about to happen next.* If just buying next to a city or town was the thing to do, you could buy anywhere within a twenty-mile radius and that could be considered a great investment. That's not the case. You've got to choose the right area within that twenty-mile radius. Liken it to buying a painting. The piece doesn't have to be painted by a currently recognised artist to be a quality piece of art. But if you're clever enough to know a good artist when you see one, the painting you buy will be worth a fortune in years to come. So don't just buy anywhere. Buy value. This is particularly important if you want to buy another property later on.

The Specifics

Answer the following questions when choosing your location:

Are there development plans for the area? Visit the local planning office and the county council website. Look for *zoned* areas.

Is there anything that might attract people, such as new employment opportunities or universities?

Is the area convenient for your work? It should be within commuting distance.

Does the area suit your lifestyle? If you like the buzz of a city, you need to be able to reach it, and if you have children, you might need an area with a good sense of community.

Are there shops close by or new ones due to open? Look for new shopping complexes. People don't open up shops if they don't see potential for good business and expansion. Well-known names indicate good future growth.

Is there good public transport in the area, or are there plans for it to be extended? If the answer is yes, the area is considered to be up-and-coming.

Are there good pubs, cafés and restaurants close by, or are there some new ones opening up? Upmarket establishments indicate upmarket residents. This will increase property prices.

Are there good schools in the area? If you have children, or intend to have them, this is important.

Are there parks and playgrounds within easy reach?

Is there a cinema or entertainment centre in the area, or is there one planned for the area within the next five years?

Is there a medical centre or hospital nearby?

Is there a bank and a post office in the area?

Is there an airport within a thirty-minute drive of the property, or is one due to open? Try to buy within driving distance of the airport but far enough away to avoid a flight path.

Are there churches, organisations, clubs and sports amenities?

The more 'yes' answers you can give to the above questions, the more likely it is that the area will be valued by other people in the future.

Tips

Ask taxi drivers about the area. They see a broad area at different times and tend to know what happened where. Also, pop into the local pub or shop and get talking to the locals.

Look out for skips and scaffolding. If people are building or renovating, you can take it that there's a good reason for it: they obviously feel that the area is worth investing in.

Know What To Avoid

A run-down area. Graffiti, derelict houses, dumped or burnt-out cars, unkempt gardens and rubbish are signs that the area is rough – probably too rough to be up-and-coming within the next five to ten years. Although these areas can be valuable to investors (we'll talk more about this later), they are not the areas in which to look for your first property.

An area with a prison or detention centre. It's likely that they'll stay there for some time and they will always put people off living there.

An area with an electricity pylon, phone mast or waste dump. They are nasty-looking things and are potentially health hazards.

An area within an airport flight path or next to a train track. They cause a heck of a lot of noise.

A busy road. This is especially relevant if you have children or want to avoid noise. Properties set back from a main road are more sought after.

An area that has been flooded. Have a look at permanent fixed measure markers.

The Building To Buy

You're not a renter any more, so the answer is not 'anything'. You have choice now, so get used to the idea.

A New House

There are many advantages to buying a new house. Firstly, banks tend to prefer them. High standards of building are expected, and they usually come with a builder's warranty. This means that the builder guarantees to fix structural faults within an agreed timeframe, usually up to ten years. For this reason, new houses are seen as a safe bet and as having good resale potential. Secondly, they are almost always centrally heated and well insulated, so maintenance is relatively low. A new fitted kitchen and bathroom suite are also usually included in the sale, so you could probably move in straight away. However, there are some drawbacks to modern properties. They usually lack character and are more expensive, although you normally get a discount if you buy the property off the plans. They tend to be smaller than older properties, and the standard pokey garden makes it difficult to extend. You also need to be aware that a developer could abandon the development before completion or could go bust. Although this is not common, it's important to be aware of it. Check that the developer has a good reputation before you hand over any money. You can do this by seeing the other developments they've completed. Ask residents about their experience of them.

An Old House

The best thing about an old house is that it has character, and if you're prepared to do some work on it you could land yourself something fantastic. Personally, I wouldn't touch anything that needs a lot of work first time around, but if you decide to take this route, make sure you get the property surveyed so that you know exactly what work will need to be done. Keep within budget, but be generous when budgeting. Hitches almost always happen along the way, and money gets eaten up quickly, especially when it comes to heating and plumbing systems. When you're viewing old properties, try to look past the flowery wallpaper, dirty carpets and stained net curtains. Think of it as an empty shell. Even if the place smells of pee, it could have huge potential. Old houses can be made to look amazing with a bit of elbow grease. They often have room to extend, which could add value later on. This is invaluable if you decide to invest further.

Tip

When buying a house, try to buy one with a 'twist'. Look for a property that has the potential for you to extend upwards or outwards (or both), that has room to put a granny flat in the back garden, or that can be divided, to make two or more properties.

An Apartment

Apartments have the advantage of being compact, and they're usually cheaper than houses. They give you a better chance of living in or very close to a city, and they're easy to maintain. They also tend to be smaller than houses, so heating and electricity bills should be lower. However, they have disadvantages too. They don't usually offer much privacy, and although there might be a common area (for which an annual maintenance fee will be required), they don't usually come with their own garden. They generally aren't suitable for anyone with a child, and there may be restrictions on the lease (such as a 'no pets' clause). Noise and lack of outside storage also need to be considered.

Tips

If you're buying an apartment, and your budget allows, try to buy on the first floor, or higher if there is an elevator. Upper floors are better when it comes to security: this is why ground-floor apartments are usually cheaper.

Think about the fact that you may let the property out in years to come. An apartment must be centrally located.

Freehold and Leasehold

If you're buying a property, you need to check if it's freehold or leasehold. Most apartments are leasehold. This means that although you own the apartment, you don't own the ground the property is built on. There's an agreement when you buy the property that you can live in it (a lease normally spans about ninety-nine years), but you'll have to pay an annual fee to the owner of the land. This fee covers the maintenance of the building and the communal areas. Most houses are freehold. This means that you own the property and you are responsible for it and its grounds. Before you sign the contract, your solicitor should find out if the property is freehold or leasehold.

Self-build

Ambitious 'property virgins' often delude themselves when it comes to building a house. They have this notion that it's as simple as looking in *Bungalow Bliss*, saying 'I want that house', and, *abracadabra*, it appears, all nice and rosy. But building a house from scratch is not for the faint-hearted. We'll discuss this more later on.

Researching the Area

Estate Agents

Pop into an estate agent's and see what's been sold in the last year. If houses in certain areas have been on the market for a long time, it's likely that they're in an undesirable area, they need work, or there's some other problem with them. Never say never, though, as they may have huge potential. You'll probably be able to haggle over the price. (We'll discuss this later too.)

Tip

Tell estate agents what you want, and outline your budget. Ask them to call you as soon as something comes up and post you information on anything they think you might be interested in. A lot of agents also have a texting system, whereby they circulate a text to update you on the latest properties. Make sure you're part of that too.

The Internet

This is probably the easiest way to do research. And it gives you something fun to do when you're meant to be working! There are loads of property websites to browse through, from the general sites, such as *daft.ie* and *my-home.ie*, to agents' individual sites. Look at both to make sure you don't miss out on anything. You'll get an idea of property prices and you'll see the latest property news.

Tip

Google-search the area, keying in words like 'drugs', 'social problems', 'vandalism', 'murders' and 'problems'.

Driving Around

Driving around an area gives you a huge amount of information. If you want to be vigilant, visit the area in the morning, in the afternoon and at about 5 PM. Checking the place out at different times will help you see what the area is like in general. You'll see how busy the place is in the morning and what it's like after school hours; in the early hours, you'll spot the lingering dodgy characters – if there are any. Check if gardens are well kept, whether the area is generally clean, and whether the cars look decent. Although this is not true in all cases, cars can tell you a lot about the area. Needless to stay, if they're burnt out it may not be the best place to buy!

Newspapers

Newspapers, especially local ones, provide a lot of information about locations and their properties. They give you the low-down on where it's all happening and where the danger zones are. If an area is bad, it will no doubt be in the headlines. Papers also have the advantage of direct contact with private sellers. Sellers often advertise properties in the classifieds in the hope of a quick sale. This cuts costs by bypassing the estate agent, and a buyer can often negotiate a better deal directly with the seller.

Tips

Sometimes properties are advertised at low prices and people automatically think it's a typo. *Always* inquire about them, because it might not be a mistake! It might just be someone who is desperate to sell.

Place an ad looking for cheap properties, something like: 'Property under €200,000 wanted. Quick sale guaranteed.' It works! Not all the time, but it does work.

Auctions

The majority of properties are sold by what's called *private treaty*, i.e. a basic seller-to-buyer sale. But some properties, especially bigger ones or one-offs, are sold at auction. I recommend that first time around you avoid buying property at auction. By all means attend one to get the low-down on the market, but never actually bid. There are two reasons for this:

1. *You're not experienced enough yet.* An auction can become heated if there are few competitors in the room. This could be disastrous for an easily influenced novice. Reserve prices (the minimum amount the property will be sold for) are not revealed before an auction. The seller sets them on the day, so if there's strong competition and the novice bidder is emotional, they could pay more for the property than it's worth. If your bid is accepted, you'll be asked to sign a contract on the spot and hand over a 10 percent deposit. If you're not able to pay, you risk forfeiting your deposit. Ouch!

2. *You'll have to pay fees even before the auction starts.* You'll need to have a solicitor ready to represent you. So let's say you went to five auctions and your bid wasn't accepted at any of them. You would have wasted a lot of money. So only go to an auction to get a feel for what it's like.

Tip

Check out town development plans. These are a blueprint for the planning and development in the area; you can get them from the county council. It's important to look at them, for a number of reasons. Firstly, you don't want to buy a property and suddenly learn that there's an abattoir being built next to you. Secondly, they'll help you to identify up-and-coming areas. Look out for things like big supermarkets, major companies and updated transport links. They all indicate predicted growth.

Property Shows

Property shows help you get a feel for the property world, but do *not* buy at them. Smiling salespeople will try to flog you something, but don't fall into the trap. They'll greet you as though you're a long-lost buddy, present you with a colourful brochure, and tell you that they have the property of the century just for you. Believe me, their little pearly grins can be very persuasive, so *never* buy on the day, even if you're tempted. Spur-of-the-moment decisions usually end in disaster. If you think you're interested in something, get the information only, and take it home with you to consider.

Buy When People Are Panicking

If you want to do well on the property ladder (which you can in any market), you've got to be on the ball, not act like a sheep. This means being clued in to what others are doing and being five steps ahead of them. It means buying quality property from scared people who are willing to sell cheap. So when you see people going frantic when they hear of a bursting property bubble, it's time for you to get excited! People who panic don't think straight. They're desperate, and will settle for a much lower price. They fear that if they don't, the bubble will pop and they'll lose out. They cut their losses. I recently bought a property and haggled the seller down from an original asking price of €185,000 to €115,000, all in. He had refused an offer €40,000 above mine five months earlier but, fearing a market crash, he panicked and decided to sell to me in case he got less later down the line.

Property prices follow trends. This is why investors don't panic when a crash is said to be imminent. We know that the market has, and always will, go up and down. Even with crashes, we know that property doubles in value roughly every seven to ten years. The general population aren't aware of this. They think short-term and get scared, especially when economists start talking about unpredictable interest rates. I wonder what would happen if people started to use their own brains. They might see solutions. Why not just fix the rate for a certain period of time!

2

Finance

So having chosen where and what to buy, it's time to get the finance. The glitch? Your piggy bank is in bad shape. Fear not, there's a way around everything. Just take action, and keep taking action, until you get what you want.

How Much Can You Afford?

I absolutely hated asking myself what I could afford to spend on a property. I didn't want to look at the likely possibility that my piggy bank was empty. But the thing is, if you want to get on the property ladder, you have to ask that question. You have to get real and be honest about your current situation, warts and all. The more honest you are with yourself now, the quicker you will get what you want. There are loads of bargains to be had, so there's no time for feeling sorry for yourself. I've drawn up a template to help you, so grab a pen and let's get right to it. Please do this exercise before reading on.

Monthly Income (after tax):

Monthly Outgoings:

Current loans:

Tax:

Insurance:

Medical:

Electricity:

Gas:

Oil:

Home phone:

Mobile phone:

Food:

Travel:

Broadband:

Cable TV:

Clothes:

Going out:

Charities:

Refuse collection:

Miscellaneous (TV licence and one-off bills):

Other luxuries (Saturday-night munchies count!):

Take away all your outgoings from your income, to give you an idea of how much money is left over at the end of the month.

TOTAL:

By any chance, does your balance sheet look awful? Chill! Mine was hopeless, really hopeless. But it's a fact – a very consoling one – that a person's income is about the same as what they spend, whether they reel in €500 a month or €50,000 a month. So if you find that what you can afford is zilch, relax. Remember, to get the best result, you've got to be realistic. Look through your outgoings list and see where you might be able to cut back. Take 15 percent off everything, even if you'd rather die. Believe it or not, you'll hardly notice. Let's face it: there are things you could live without for a while. Could you survive without cable TV? Could you use your legs to get from A to B rather than driving? Could you skip the lattes?

The Deposit

The bank will normally lend a first-time buyer about 90 percent of the property purchase price; you have to come up with the other 10 percent, *the deposit.* This hurdle – and it is just a hurdle – is probably the main reason people back away from the property ladder. 'I can't afford it' is the usual response. The real question should be: 'How can I afford it?' Not having it in your bank account is not a reason to give up. How many people do you know with a stash in their bank account that would cover 10 percent of a property? I don't know many.

Start to get creative. Look for alternatives.

Going Joint

A lot of people presume that they have to go it alone (or with a partner) when they are looking to buy a house. But banks are actually happy to lend to two or more people wanting to buy together as long as the people buying are reliable. You must make sure that your relationship with the person you're buying with has stood the test of time. Reliability is key. To safeguard yourself against any possible hiccups, get a *co-ownership agreement* drawn up. A solicitor will draw one up for about €150–200. It's not a compulsory agreement but you'd be nuts not to have one. This document keeps everything simple. It states the terms of ownership (how much of the property each person owns, and so on) so that everything is clear from day one. Some people, especially unmarried couples, have a problem with co-ownership agreements, and I guess that's understandable. It's like saying that I'm going to cover my ass in case we break up, presupposing a lack of confidence in the longevity of the relationship. But that's just stupid. Buying property is a business transaction and has nothing to do with the quality of a relationship. Common sense should prevail.

Tip

Always make sure there's an exit strategy in place in the agreement. This should be written into the contract so that if any of you want to get out of the deal, you can.

Example of Going Joint

You and two others, maybe family or friends, decide to buy a place together. Let's say that you need €30,000 for a deposit but none of you can afford to front up the whole amount on their own.

Think Outside the Box

Could you split the deposit three ways? For a property costing €300,000, for instance, you would only have to come up with €10,000 each.

Would the others be prepared to put up the deposit between them on the condition that you pay a bit extra towards the mortgage every month? At some point, the property could be sold to an outsider, or you could buy the others out. They will get their deposit back in full. Over time, the house should go up in value and the sale proceeds could be split. Not only will they get their deposit back, you should all end up with a profit. You could use your part as a deposit on your own house!

Sell something. Do you have a car or something else that's worth a few bob? Prioritise.

Family Members

Would a family member be prepared to give you the deposit on the condition you pay them back? This might be via monthly payment (with or without interest) or a lump sum on an agreed date (maybe through an equity release, which I will talk about later on). You could draw up a private contract to state the terms.

Tip

If you have savings, make sure they're in a good interest-paying account until you need to use the money.

One Hundred Percent Mortgages

Some financial institutions used to lend 100 percent of the purchase price of a property, generally to people with 'secure' employment (teachers, doctors, accountants and so on). (For an investment property, this allowed you to finance the entire purchase price of the investment property without having to come up with the deposit in cash.) But with the bursting of the property bubble, lenders have tightened their belts, and these mortgages are generally no longer available.

The rule should be: push for as much as you can get, but only borrow what you can afford to repay. And if you're an invesetor, *never* take out a 100 percent mortgage unless you're sure the property is worth *more* than the mortgage you're getting against it. You don't want to be in a situation of negative equity, i.e. stuck with a property that, if you needed to sell, wouldn't cover the mortgage owed on it. This is another reason to buy under-market-value properties. You reduce the risk of negative equity straight away.

Schemes

There are lots of schemes to help finance a mortgage, and they're definitely worth looking into. I wasn't eligible for any of these schemes, but I would like to have been!

Affordable Housing Scheme

In 1999, the government set up a scheme that allowed certain first-time buyers to purchase new properties below market value (i.e. for less than the property would fetch on the open market). The scheme was designed for people who couldn't afford to buy a property at market value but who earned too much to be part of a social housing scheme (see below). Since 2000, developers have had to make 20 percent of their developments available for sale at cost price – which is sometimes as little as 50 percent of the property's market value.

If you want to apply for affordable housing, you can download an application form from *www.affordable-home.ie*. If you're eligible, send in your form to the relevant county council. Then it's a matter of waiting with your fingers and toes crossed. To use the lottery phrase: *It could be you!* As you can, imagine people wanting to live in Dublin city have the worst odds of getting a property under this scheme. So if you want to live near the big smoke, apply to Fingal County Council. The odds are better. If you apply for housing outside Dublin, the odds are better again.

Certain lending institutions entered into an affordable-housing agreement with the Department of the Environment, Heritage and Local Government. If you are accepted for the scheme, you'll take out a mortgage with one of these institutions. The loan can be anything up to 97 percent of the property price (the average mortgage is 90 to 92 percent for first-timers) but repayments can't be any higher than 35 percent of the household's net income. The amount you get depends on your circumstances.

Social Housing: Shared Ownership Scheme

This scheme works well for a lot of people, but there's a waiting list. The scheme was set up for people with low to middle incomes who wouldn't get a mortgage with a regular lending institution. (In a single-income household, your gross income must be less than €40,000 for you to be eligible for the scheme. In a two-income household, multiply the higher income by 2.5 and add the lower income; if the total is less than €100,000, you are eligible.) Any property qualifies for the scheme as long as the price is realistic, the property is structurally sound and it's big enough. The local authority funds the mortgage and the interest rates are fairly low. The idea is that you pay part mortgage payments and part rent to the council for an agreed period. You'll initially own at least 40 percent of the property and you'll rent the rest until you can afford to buy the council out. You can buy the rented share in full at any time or you can buy shares as you go along, using cash or by topping up the mortgage. You'll be asked to do this within twenty-five years of becoming part of the scheme. If you want to sell the house at any time, you are entitled to do so, but if you got the property at a discount to start with, you have to refund the council a percentage of the profit made from the resale. If you sell the property in the first ten years of occupancy, you have to refund the whole discount. A reduction of 10 percent a year is given for each year of occupancy between ten and twenty years. After twenty years of full occupancy, no refund is required. You become the full owner of the property after thirty years. (You may need to borrow more money to pay off the balance at this stage.)

Tax Incentive Housing

A few years ago, the government came up with a juicy carrot to entice people to buy in areas that are in need of improvement. They developed a plan whereby good income tax concessions (spread over a period of ten years) were given for people who bought properties in certain areas (mostly run-down inner-city and rural areas). The following are the main categories:

Urban Renewal Scheme

This was introduced in 1985 in an attempt to combat the increasing problem of dilapidated and derelict buildings in inner-city areas, especially areas that had suffered population decline. To ensure that priority was given to the areas with the greatest need for renewal, *integrated area plans* had to be drawn up for each area, i.e. the overall development plan policies and aims could be incorporated into more detailed plans. Areas that are part of the scheme include parts of Waterford, Cork, Galway and Limerick.

Rural Renewal Scheme

This scheme is designated to areas that have experienced long-term population decline and poor economic growth, such as Longford, Leitrim and parts of Roscommon, Cavan and Sligo. The scheme aims to attract people back into rural areas to ease overpopulation in cities.

Town Renewal Scheme

This scheme is designated to towns with populations of between 500 and 6,000. The objective is to make living in a town more appealing. In this regard, older buildings are restored, and commercial, leisure and social activities are promoted.

Living Over the Business Scheme

This scheme was set up to encourage refurbishment of vacant upper storeys in existing buildings for residential use. It also involves the designation of Enterprise Areas in order to attract technology-based industries. Areas in Cork, Limerick, Galway, Dublin and Waterford qualify.

Tip

A property bought under one of the above schemes could prove to be worthwhile investment. The designated areas are to be developed, so if you get in at the early stages, you could own something very valuable in a few years' time.

Home Choice Loan

This scheme is for first-time buyers who can afford to buy a property (which is new or self-build) on the open market and can afford to pay a mortgage but can't get enough cash from a bank or building society to buy the property. If at least two lenders turn you down for finance and you can get a registered broker to confirm it, this scheme might be for you. If you qualify, you can get a loan up to €285,000 and, depending on income, up to

92 percent loan to value is available. The loan term is up to thirty years.

To qualify, you must meet the following criteria:

Be a first-time buyer (some exceptions may apply)

Earn a minimum of €40,000 as a single applicant and over €50,000 as joint applicants.

Be in permanent employment for two years, with two years' certified accounts if you're self-employed.

Have broker confirmation of being refused finance.

The property must be in the Republic of Ireland.

Rent-to-buy Scheme

This innovative scheme is essentially a try-before-you-buy scheme. Basically, you choose a property, rent it for a a fixed monthly payment and, after a specified period (up to three years), you have the option to buy the property or walk away. The great thing about this scheme is that you don't need to fork out a hefty deposit (you only need €2,995 plus VAT). And the rent you paid along the way is credited against the price of the property when you eventually buy it. Also, it gives you the opportunity to see whether the property is right for you – and to show the lender that you can maintain payments.

Rent a Room Scheme

This is a scheme everyone can benefit from, you included. If you don't mind someone living in your gaff, you should definitely go for it. It's a scheme whereby you, as an owner-occupier, can rent out a room in your property. You are entitled to receive tax relief on €10,000 in rent payments, reducing your mortgage payments as a result. The bank takes this into account when looking at your repayment capacity for a mortgage.

Digs

Although not a scheme as such, I thought I'd slot this little money-earner in here to show you that there are ways to gather money to pay a mortgage. Digs basically involves taking in a student, almost as a family member, for a weekly or monthly fee. The only drawback is that you might have to be around to cook for them, do their laundry, and so on. If you're working from home (a good way to save money), you might be able to swing this one easily enough. Worth considering.

Tip

Any time you take in a lodger, make sure you interview them, ask for references and set house rules from the start. If the tenant is young, get a guarantee from their parents to ensure that the rent will be paid.

Where There's a Will, There's a Way

Banks have policies whereby they only lend a certain percentage of the property price. Therefore, whether they think you can afford 100 percent or more, if it's not their policy, they probably won't sanction it. So if you don't have the money and the bank won't give it to you, you could be tempted to give up. Please don't. There's a solution to every problem if you look long enough. For example, some people get second jobs or create new businesses to generate more cash. Some save more every month in high-interest paying accounts. Think outside the box and you'll get ideas. But keep it legal!

Note

Disabled Person's Grant

If you're buying a home and you (or perhaps your partner) have special needs, you can get a Disabled Person's Grant. This grant covers the cost of adapting a home and could save you huge amounts of money if you qualify. The money is granted for structural repairs or improvements such as re-wiring, installing of central heating, water and sanitary services, radon remediation, dry-lining, repairs to or replacement of window and doors, contract cleaning and painting. You can find out more about this grant on your county council website.

The Bank

Will the Bank Work Out What I Can Afford?

The bank wants to be sure they'll get their money back eventually, so they do a few calculations before giving you a cent. They look at your income and your job. (If you have qualifications, this might boost your chances of getting more money, so make sure to shove them under the bank manager's nose.) They will also not want you to be paying more than 35 to 40 percent of your disposable income on debt repayments (see the section on Stress Testing below).

Things the Bank Considers

1) YOUR JOB

How long have you been employed? The longer the better. It shows you're committed. If you're on social welfare, you'll need to start earning and be in full-time employment for about six months for banks to feel happy lending you money.

Is your job permanent or part-time? Is it likely to stay that way? Permanent jobs make banks feel more secure. A letter from your employer to verify future permanent employment goes a long way. This would be especially beneficial to you if you've been on social welfare.

What is your annual salary after tax? They'll look at extra income, overtime, commission, bonuses and second jobs. So start buttering up the boss. Although not all lenders take bonuses into consideration, they do increase your chances of getting finance.

Are you self-employed? If you are, the amount you can borrow will depend on how good your books are. They'll ask for three years' business accounts and a copy of your tax clearance certificate.

2) Your Commitments

Do you have children? How many? They're expensive little creatures.

Do you have loans? How many, and when are they due to be cleared?

3) Your Current Rent Payments

If the amount of rent you pay is close to what the mortgage payment would be, it shows that you have the ability to make payments. If you paid your rent by direct debit, you should show the bank the statement. You should also get your landlord to write a letter to verify your good payment record. The lender may not ask for either, but give it to them anyway.

Stress Testing

Your repayment capacity will be *stress tested* before the bank agrees to give you a mortgage. This is a standard quick calculation process and nothing to worry about. It just means that the bank will test your ability to handle the repayments if interest rates rise. The test is now normally based on a 2.75 percent rise. If they're happy you can manage the payments, everything's hunky dory. You can do your own stress test before you go looking for money if you want, so you know the mortgage payments that are realistic for you. You'll find the current mortgage rates in the newspaper. Look at the APR (Annualised Percentage Rate) of interest – the true cost of a loan) and add 3 percent. If you're happy you can pay this amount, you'll feel more secure.

What Type of Mortgage?

So what type of mortgage should you go for? I found the mortgage jargon a bit confusing. Actually, *very* confusing! It has to be the greatest load of technical babble I ever heard. I've made it simple for you.

Annuity Mortgage

The fancy name aside, this mortgage is simply one where you pay the money borrowed (known as capital) and the interest charged on it. It's the most common type of mortgage. Sometimes it's called a *capital and interest mortgage.* For the first few years, your monthly payment is mostly interest. Towards the end of the mortgage term, you'll be paying off mostly capital.

Interest-only Mortgage

You pay only the interest on the mortgage for an agreed period. The bank expects that after the agreed period, you'll pay them back in full. The time period for interest-only mortgages varies from bank to bank, and only a few offer this type of mortgage to first-time buyers. This is worth looking into if you intend to use it as an investment property. It gives you a bit of financial breathing space starting off. Investors favour interest-only mortgages as they maximise the monthly cash flow (the money left over from any rental income after the mortgage payments are covered) as they rent it out.

Current-account Mortgage

With a current-account mortgage, your monthly payments are linked to your current account. This means that whatever money is in your account, even if it's only there for a short period, will go towards your mortgage payments. That sounds OK considering that the loan will be paid off quicker, saving you money in the long term. The problem, which some people might see as an advantage at first, is that you can borrow from the equity in the property (the difference between your mortgage and the value of the property) when you want. Suddenly your mortgage account becomes a holiday or clothes fund. Disaster!

Interest Rates

I'm sure you've heard people talking about *fixing* their mortgage payments because of the current volatility in interest rates set by the ECB (the European Central Bank). But what exactly does 'fixing' mean? Well, for an agreed period, usually between one and ten years, your mortgage payments will remain the same every month, a bit like renting. The advantage of this is that you have peace of mind: your payments will not be affected if interest rates go up. Fixing may make you feel more secure. The downside is that if interest rates go down – and they are on a downward slide at the moment – you still have to pay the agreed fixed rate.

For this reason, some people go for a *variable rate.* These rates are generally a little cheaper than fixed rates and they offer more flexibility if rates change. The disadvantage is that you won't know what your payments will be from one month to the next. (Until recently, a *tracker rate* mortgage was another option. The rate 'tracks' – i.e. is tied to – the ECB rate. These mortgages have been popular in the past but at the time of writing are no longer available in Ireland.)

What To Do?

It's up to you really, and it depends on how much security you want. I tend to fix my mortgages (as long as the rate is good). I like to feel secure. Interest rates are low at the moment but may rise. Fixing all or part of the mortgage may be your best option. If you fix, do so for two to three years. If interest rates come down, you won't get stung too badly, but if they go up, you'll benefit.

The Repayment Term

Next, you need to decide on your repayment term. I wanted to keep my repayments to a minimum every month, so I stretched the mortgage over thirty years. Some banks will give you a forty-year mortgage, depending on your age and other factors. But because repayments are stretched over a longer period, it means that you end up paying more interest to the bank. By the time you finish this book, you'll realise that this is not something to get your knickers in a twist over, especially if you decide to invest further!

Research the Market

It's important to research the market before you take out a mortgage. You should also make sure you're getting the best rate available from whoever you decide to go with, as they offer a range of different packages. And remember that the bank is trying to sell you a product, not trying to be your friend. A bank is a business institution, not a person; it's an institution that sells money packages. I found that idea hard to grasp at first. I didn't see the bank as selling me something. It felt as though they were doing me a favour by giving me a mortgage. I just wanted cash to buy my house, and to be honest I was damn glad that anyone would give it to me. But the fact is that you're keeping the bank in business.

Deferring Payments

I deferred making my first payment for three months, and you'll probably have the option to do the same. I didn't want to be strapped for cash as soon as I moved into my house. The thought of sitting on a cardboard box eating beans didn't appeal to me. The way it works is that you make an agreement with the bank to start making payments on a set date after you draw down the mortgage. So let's say you draw down the mortgage in May: you could start payments in August. This breathing space makes life so much easier, allowing you to kit out your home.

Mortgage Fees

Brokerage Fee

Some people prefer to use a mortgage broker starting off. A broker basically does the work for you, liaising with the bank on your behalf. But remember that they get commission for signing you up and don't mind which bank gives them the commission, as long as they get it. For this reason, it might be worth paying for an independent broker who acts solely for you. You'll pay for it, but at least they'll have your interests at heart. They'll touch base with all the lending institutions, check what's on offer, and try to get you the best deal. The fee charged is often a flat fee of a few hundred euro, but some ask for a percentage of the mortgage. If you're thinking of using a particular broker, ask around and get a recommendation from someone who has used them before and was happy with the result.

Tip

Never use a mortgage broker who is also acting as the estate agent for the property you are buying. They may have a conflict of interest.

Insurance

Life Cover

The bank will ask you to get life insurance just in case you die before the mortgage is paid in full. They might recommend a company, but get quotes from a few companies before deciding on anything. When you've found the company that offers the best deal, you should go a step further and haggle over the price, even if it's is the lowest on the market. With some negotiation, you'll get it cheaper. Sometimes merely saying 'I'm sure you can do better than that' gets you a reduction. Most people trying to get a reduction do the 'Another company offered me a better deal' thing, but the fact is that most companies know what their competitors are charging, so don't bother using that tactic. Use a genuine haggling tool. For example, you'll need to get home insurance, so tell them that if they give you a reduction for life cover, you'll buy the home policy with them. Another way to get a reduction is to tell them that you're an investor. They know that you'll need insurance on the other properties too.

Payment Protection Insurance (Critical Illness Cover)

This is optional insurance. It covers you if you get ill and can't meet the mortgage repayments. Your payments will be covered for a few months, depending on how long you have the mortgage. This form of insurance can be expensive, though, and a claim can be difficult to make successfully.

House Insurance

You'll need to get your house and its contents insured in case of theft, fire, flooding, and so on. Again, suss out a few companies to get the best deal. And *always* tell them you want a better deal or you'll go elsewhere. This has always worked for me – so much so that I usually get my insurance for about a third less than most people. Ask and you will usually receive. Be cheeky and you will always receive. Payments can be paid monthly or as an annual sum but, depending on the company, further discounts may be given for a lump-sum payment.

Sums

Now it's time to do some more totting up. The itty-bitty expenses add up, so account for them now. Have a look at the list below and fill in the blanks. You might not understand some of the terms, but I will explain them later. Leave the bits you don't understand and fill them in later.

Ten percent deposit on property:

Monthly mortgage payment:

Arrangement fee:

Life cover:

Mortgage protection:

Solicitor's fee:

Surveyor's fee:

Valuation fee:

Property insurance:

Land Registry:

Local authority search:

Council tax:

Van hire for removal:

TOTAL:

Mortgage Tax Relief

Anyone who gets a mortgage on their main home can apply to the Revenue Commissioners for Mortgage Tax Relief on the mortgage interest paid. It's granted at source by the lending institution and is in the form of either a reduced monthly mortgage payment or as a credit to your account. It's up to you to claim it, though. To do this, you need to get a TRS1 (Tax Relief at Source 1) form from the Revenue Commissioners (*revenue.ie*), complete it and return it to them. As a first-time buyer, you're entitled to a higher rate for the first seven years of your mortgage. (This stands even if you decide to change house or bank, or re-mortgage your home.) The rate of tax relief is 25 percent for the first two years, 22.5 percent for the third, fourth and fifth years, and 20 percent for the sixth and seventh years. For non-first-time buyers, the rate of tax relief is 15 percent.

Tip

If you decide to top up your mortgage later on, *remember to reapply for tax relief.* It's not issued automatically.

The Mortgage Application

What Will the Bank Ask For?

Keep this simple and organised. When I got my first mortgage, I was so sloppy, giving the bank the documents in dribs and drabs all over the place. Collect the documents you need, as outlined below, and put them neatly in a folder. You want the bank to take you seriously from the beginning. An organised person indicates organised mortgage payments.

Tip

The folder should be bound and each page headed.

page 1
'MORTGAGE PROPOSAL'

page 2
Applicant's Name:
Applicant's Phone Number (home and mobile):
Applicant's Address:
Solicitor's Name and Contact Details:
Accountant's Name and Contact Details:

page 3
'PROPERTY FOR WHICH FINANCE IS REQUIRED'
Details and photograph if available

page 4
PHOTOGRAPHIC PROOF OF IDENTIFICATION
To prove you are who you say you are. Photocopies rather than the actual documents are usually OK.

page 5
PROOF OF ADDRESS
Two utility bills (e.g. phone statement, electricity statement or gas statement)

page 6
BANK STATEMENTS
Most banks will ask for three to six months of statements. Provide six months' worth.

page 7
PROOF OF EMPLOYMENT AND TAX AFFAIRS
If you're employed, include a letter from your employer to verify your employment and the terms of your employment. If you're self-employed, include three years' business accounts, a breakdown of your earnings and your most recent P60 form. If you don't have a P60, include a letter from your accountant to say that your

tax affairs are up to date. You could also provide a tax return to prove that you are tax-compliant.

page 8
CURRENT LOAN DETAILS

If you have any outstanding loans, such as a car loan, a student loan or credit card borrowing, include six months' statements to show that you have a good payment record. The bank likes to see a good credit history. In addition to the statements, you should include a credit report. This is a document held by the Irish Credit Bureau (ICB) detailing information about you and your borrowings. The details are held in the form of a report for five years after any loan is closed.

The report includes:

Your name, date of birth and address

Account numbers of current loans and loans that were active within the last five years

The names of the lenders involved with the loan

Monthly repayments or missed payments

Failure to pay off a loan

Loans that were settled for less than was initially agreed

Legal actions taken against you

The bank runs a credit check on any borrower, but including the report in your folder makes their life easier. Needless to say, don't include the report if you know your credit history is bad.

Bad Credit

Let's face it: lenders don't like a poor credit history. The borrower is considered to be a higher risk. But all is not lost if you didn't pay your bills in the past. There are a few lenders, known as sub-prime lenders, who do mortgages for people with a poor credit history. Interest rates are higher, but if you're serious about getting on the property ladder and you've learned from past mistakes, you can do it. After a few years, your improved credit rating means you can switch to a different lender.

Tip

If you defaulted on a loan, arrange for the loan to be paid off over a longer term with smaller payments. Then when you apply for a mortgage, get a letter to verify the arrangement.

What Should You Do If You Can't Meet the Payments?

If you follow the advice in this book, you'll never have to ask that question. But in the unlikely event that you can't meet the repayments, you should contact your lender straight away. If they know the score, arrangements can be made. You can also contact the Department of Social Welfare about MABS (the Money and Budgeting Advice Service) or your local St Vincent de Paul Society.

3

The Buying Process

OK, you've submitted your mortgage application. All going well you'll be made an *offer in principle*. That is, the bank will agree to give you a mortgage on the condition that the property you choose is worth the price. Make sure you arrange a mortgage in principle before you look at any property. You'll avoid the head-wrecking experience of trying to get finance when the right property turns up, and you make yourself more attractive to a seller.

Once your mortgage has been approved in principle, write down your criteria when it comes to buying property. I didn't realise the importance of this when I was buying my first place, but now, knowing how easy it is to get sucked in by the excitement of buying property, especially the first one, I know it's crucial. If you write down the type of property you want, you're more likely to stick to the criteria, be logical and make a good decision. Agents love first-time buyers because they know they can pull on their heartstrings. You must not get sucked in, even if they associate a wonderful lifestyle with the property, as is the case with show houses. View at least ten properties before making a decision, and only buy if the deal makes sense.

Viewing

Set up viewing appointments, and whatever you do, find out the seller's circumstances. Investors always do this. It gives us bargaining power. Ask why the property is being sold and how long it has been on the market, even if this seems cheeky or nosey. Knowing the seller's circumstances will give you an idea of how desirable the property is, which determines what your bargaining power is. Are they due to move into another property soon and in a hurry to sell? Are they going through a divorce or moving country? Are they in trouble with their lender? If the answer to any of those questions is yes, you have good bargaining power. *Always* look for bargaining power.

Tip

Find out if the seller has changed agents, and for what reason. If an agent can't shift the property, it might indicate a lack of interest in it among potential buyers.

Be on time for the viewing, have a mobile phone with you, and tell someone where you're going (for reasons of personal safety). Bring a pen and paper to record the condition of the property. It's easy to forget what properties are like after you've left them. Use the template below as a guide. Fill in the boxes and review each property at home later over a cuppa. *Never* agree to a sale on the spur of the moment. Record and review, and buy only if the property meets your criteria. If none of the properties meet your criteria, don't buy. Something will turn up. If you do happen to find a property that fits your criteria, however, set up a second viewing and inspect the property in more detail. If it shapes up, you can think about making an offer.

Property record no.:

Built date:

Reason for sale:

Urgency of sale/motivated seller:

Asking price:

Number of bedrooms:

Rate on a scale of 1 (terrible) to 10 (excellent):

The Exterior

Driveway

Garden

Parking Is it private and off-road, or are there parking restrictions?

Brickwork and mortar Re-pointing brickwork can be costly.

Roof Broken tiles and slates will need to be fixed.

Plaster

Windows Are they double-glazed and are the frames in good condition?

Drains Are the gutters the new plastic type or the old metal ones? Are they leak-free?

Pathways

Trees If they're close to the house, they could cause problems with foundations.

Existing extension quality If it's like an icebox compared to the rest of the house, chances are the insulation isn't great.

Is there room for an extension?

Any past planning applications refused?

Nearby rivers or streams that could cause flooding?

The view

Possible charges involved (applicable to apartments)

The Interior

Plaster Crumbly?

Electrics How old?

Plumbing Are the water pipes made of lead? This is a health hazard.

Heating system Type? Old or new?

Kitchen

Bathroom

Special features Are there period fireplaces, sash windows, cornicing and so on?

Windows Type and condition

Storage

Attic space Room for conversion?

Room size A bedroom should have room for a bed!

Floors If they're springy under your feet, it may be a sign of dry rot, a fungus which can spread and which could hit your pocket hard.

Insulation Single or double?

Woodwork Are there signs of woodworm? You will recognise this by the appearance of clusters of small holes.

Habitability Can you move in straight away?

Other faults

Note

The property doesn't have to be perfect. If it's structurally sound, it could be fixed up. Take note of what needs to be done, work out how much it will cost (a surveyor can estimate this for you) and factor it into your budget.

Inspect everything, even the attic, especially if the property is more than thirty years old. The water tank could be damaged or the rafters could be rotten. Don't be put off if the estate agent or the seller is awkward about it. After all, it could be your home. And besides, they could be trying to hide faults. Some people would sell you a flea-infested shack if they thought you'd buy it. If needs be, politely ask them to leave while you have a nose around. It's easier to inspect a property if you don't have someone breathing over your shoulder. After you've done your second viewing inspection, you could ask for receipts or guarantees for work carried out on the property, for things like wiring and a damp-proof course (DPC).

Tip

When viewing, imagine each room as being an empty white-walled room. This helps you see what could be done with the property.

Look at the ceilings in each room. Brown patches indicate damp: the water tank may be damaged.

The Valuation

Before making an offer, you'll need to have the property valued. The bank will insist on a valuation before approving a loan anyway, and they will have a list of valuers they use regularly. They want to confirm that the property is worth the purchase price. You'll have to cough up for it, though, whether you go through with the sale or not. Unfair, I know, but it can't be avoided. It'll set you back around €130.

Tip

Find out what valuers are on the lender's list. Ask around to see who tends to give the highest valuation, and request that valuer.

The Survey

A survey usually isn't necessary on a new property, as they come with a home bond warranty or guarantee. But if you're buying a second-hand property, get it surveyed. This will cost a few hundred euro, depending on who does it, but it's worth the money. Buying a property without having a survey done isn't recommended. Problems like dry rot, rising damp, subsidence, brick damage and creepy-crawly woodworm can easily go unnoticed when viewing the property. Any property can be dolled up with a lick of paint and a few fluffy cushions. Be vigilant. Look past the glitz and concentrate on the structure of the building. If you decide to place an offer on the property, make it subject to survey.

The Surveyor's Report

The surveyor will look at the property's structure and will identify any faults. They should be linked to a professional organisation and be able to do a proper examination. They'll put the information in a report for you, but you will need to read it slowly and thoroughly. If there are any confusing bits, ask someone (the surveyor themself, perhaps) to go through it with you.

Negotiating the Asking Price

If you're buying a new property or a property off the plans, negotiating the price is usually not an option, although if you buy a property off the plans, you usually get a discount. But if you're buying a second-hand property, always negotiate the price. Estate agents mark up the property price on purpose with the expectation that you'll try to negotiate it down. To increase your chances of getting the seller to knock down the price, find their weakness. For example, are they desperate to sell? Put yourself in their shoes. What would make you agree to a reduction? Find something negative about the property that will justify a cheaper price. Complaining about the colour of the paint on the walls won't cut it, so find solid leverage – something you can use as a bargaining tool. If there's any structural work to be done, for example, use that. If the windows are ropey or the kitchen needs changing, point it out. If a new heating or water system is needed, point that out. During the viewing, voice all the faults you notice, and don't look eager to buy. That way the agent won't be surprised when you offer les than the asking price. If they ask you what you think at the time, tell them you 'have to do the numbers to see if the deal makes sense'.

Making an Offer

If you decide you want to buy a property, think about placing an offer. You don't need to write a formal letter; a phone call will do. The *typical* (not mine or yours!) first offer is usually about 5 to 10 percent below the asking price but, after some haggling, the actual price paid is usually somewhere between the asking price and the offer. This will depend on the demand for the property and how desperate the seller is to get rid of it. It will also depend on what the property is actually worth. Find out. Don't just believe what you're told it's worth. Check the sale price, not the asking price, of similar properties in the area. You want to get the property at a rock-bottom price, so the more you know, the better.

When you're placing an offer, never offer the asking price, even if you've read elsewhere that you should. Unless you absolutely love the property, you're sure it's worth the asking price, and there's already a high bid in on it, always offer *much less* than the asking price. You should set the price, not them. Most people think that a seller will automatically refuse an offer (and usually they do initially), but remember, if you offer a high price and they accept, you'll never know if they would have accepted less. The agent is obliged to present your offer to the seller, no matter how low it is, so even if the agent laughs at your initial bid, don't raise it unless the seller refuses. Never ever bid against yourself. Offer low, and don't let the agent or the seller know that you might bid higher if they reject your offer. If your offer is rejected, wait a week or two to see if they change their mind. They may just be playing you to see if you offer more. Hold back, be patient and play them. They will often retract their refusal!

Tip

If your first offer is refused, note the length of time the seller took to refuse. If they took a while, they probably toyed with the idea of accepting your offer, so they are close to backing down. If the offer is refused straight away, on the other hand, you might have to negotiate.

Gazumping

You may have heard someone telling you that they were gazumped. But what does it mean? Basically, when a seller who has already accepted your offer decides to accept a higher offer from another buyer, you have been gazumped. I know: don't people have a heart? When it comes to making cash, they don't. Gazumping could happen at any point before the contract is exchanged, and it's completely legal in this country. It's not that common, but it does happen. It can't happen on a new home (after you've paid a deposit) but it can on a second-hand property. Until the contract is signed, neither of you has to buy or sell. Unfortunately, if the seller decides to accept the higher bid from someone else, you won't be reimbursed for any surveys and valuations you've already paid for. To reduce the chances of being gazumped, always request that the property be taken off the market, and then exchange the contracts as soon as possible. You can arrange an *exclusivity agreement*, whereby the seller signs an agreement stating that for an agreed time they won't sell the property to anyone else. However, usually getting it off the market does the job.

The Deposit

If the sale is *agreed*, you'll be asked to front up a booking deposit for the property. This is security for the seller that you're not going to dump the sale. It's usually anything up to about 5 percent of the selling price. However, there is a way around this, but most people don't know about it. You can buy a property with no money down. I do this by getting my solicitor to give the agent a written undertaking that the deposit will be paid to them when the mortgage funds are drawn down and, with finance approved in principal, I show them my formal letter of offer. They usually feel secure enough with that.

Once that's done, the sale contract will be drawn up and your solicitor will forward 10 percent of the purchase price (the booking deposit is included in this) to the seller's solicitor.

Tip

Make sure to get the property with no money down, as this gives you breathing space.

Finding a Solicitor

I can't emphasise enough how important it is to get a good solicitor. Employ one who's been recommended to you by friends or family, and whom they have used for a property purchase. The buying process needs to be as smooth as possible for you, and a poor solicitor could potentially make your life hell. Don't employ one just because they're cheap. They could end up costing more money in the long run. Employ one who gives a top-notch service, even if they cost a bit more. They should have your sole interests in mind, be efficient, and be able to explain everything to you in layman's terms, including the jargon in the sale contract. Believe me, you'll need them to: contract language is in a league of its own! They should also be contactable and should return calls or emails promptly.

Tip

If you intend to buy more property later on, let your solicitor know. They'll probably give you a better rate.

Ask your solicitor if their fees can be paid in two instalments, one after the sale and another two months down the line, rather than the whole amount at once. They should be OK with that if they know they will be paid. This gives you more breathing space.

Your Solicitor's Job

Your solicitor will handle the sale from start to finish. They'll carry out *searches* for you. These include things like Good Title (to make sure the previous owner has sole ownership of the property), Land Registry (a property has to be registered with the government to be sold), use of the land before the house was built (for example, if it was previously used for landfill or as a graveyard) and any planned developments for the area (phone masts, planned motorways, and so on). They will make sure that there are no debts on the property and confirm that the property has the right building licences and planning-permission certificates (called a certificate of compliance) for work carried out on the property.

Tip

Try to get the seller to include any decent furniture or fixtures in the sale. They often will, because it saves them having to get rid of them (if they intend to buy new stuff) or store them. Make sure that your solicitor writes this into the contract.

Check if there were any boundary disputes with neighbours and if planning permission was ever refused for anything. You want the new neighbours to like you, so have any differences ironed out from the start.

Snagging

If you're buying a new property, your solicitor will advise you to carry out a *snag* before signing the final contract. This is usually more applicable to new properties than second-hand ones. Basically, it means going through the property with a fine-tooth comb to make sure that everything is up to scratch for the handover. Be really picky and write *everything*, no matter how small, on the list. Even if there is a screw loose, get it fixed. When the builders are off-site, they *won't* return to fix bad plasterwork, scratched windows, botched paint jobs or anything else. Get it all done before you hand over your cash. There are things that I regret not having put right in the first house I bought. I got over-excited and wanted to get into my house as soon as I could. I pushed the bad workmanship aside. It's the things you say 'Ah, it'll be fine' about that later annoy you.

Tips for Snagging

Bring a torch with you. Bulbs are rarely fitted in new houses, so it can be hard to see flaws. Shine the torch at an angle over the plasterwork to make sure it's smooth.

Always concentrate on one room at a time. People have a habit of wandering from room to room when ideas come into their heads. Take your time and have a separate list for each room.

Bring a hairdryer to make sure the sockets work.

Bring a light bulb to test the fittings.

Be on good terms with the builders. They will do the work quicker for someone who is nice.

Once you're happy that all's in order, the final contract will be drawn up. It will contain general information about property sales and some information relevant to your property. The seller's solicitor will send two copies of the contract to your solicitor, and if you're happy with them you will sign both. Your solicitor will keep one and send the other back to the seller's solicitor for the seller to sign. The contracts will then be exchanged, and your solicitor will forward the outstanding finance to the seller's solicitor. Then you get the keys! The whole process, from signing the contract to completion of the sale, takes anything from four weeks to a few months.

Tips

Make sure you ask for all *the keys.* That includes: front and back doors, shed and garage doors, gates, exterior meter-cupboard door and window locks. If the property is in an apartment block, you'll need to get the main entrance door key, the entrance code and the electric-gate opener, if applicable.

Put a coloured, labelled fob on each key to help you remember which key is for which door.

Get the alarm code if an alarm is fitted and change the code on handover.

Stalling

Sometimes the seller's solicitor might hold things up. Keep on the ball and get your solicitor to check why. The seller might be negotiating with another buyer, having problems getting into their new property, or having second thoughts about moving. It's your responsibility to keep track of what's going on.

Paying your solicitor

After the sale has taken place, you'll have to pay your solicitor. The cost is, on average, 1.5 percent of the property price, but ask if they'll do it for less. Find out what you'll be charged before any work is started, and make sure you get the quote in writing.

Land Registry

The property needs to be registered in your name by law. This will cost about €700, and it's payable after the sale has gone through.

4

Self-build

Building your own property and seeing the finished product feels great, but both the pros and cons need to be considered before you decide to go down this road. On the plus side, you get to design it, so you can give the property character. And it normally works out cheaper than a similar built property. But on the negative side, it is a hands-on process that can get very messy if you don't know what you're doing or if you don't employ professionals who do. You need to have a cool head, good conflict-resolution skills, an ability to manage finances and a good tolerance for stress. How smooth the process is depends on who you employ to do the work, who manages the project and the amount of support you get along the way. Always get advice from someone who has done it before.

Finding a Site

Although this is a bit harder than it was thirty years ago, if you look hard enough it is still possible to get a good site. And apart from applications for monstrosities, most planning applications are accepted. Don't be put off by what people say about refused planning permission. Sometimes a few little adjustments to the property design will be required, but normally it's nothing major. So if your design blends in with the area, it should be fine. The main thing for you to remember is to buy the site *subject to planning permission.* If your planning application is refused, you won't have lost anything except the application fee (€49 for outline planning permission). 'Subject to planning permission' just means that you agree to buy the site only if planning is approved for the building you want.

Planning Permission

Every five years, a town council will review the town's development plan. The council looks at the general area and decides what (if anything) should go where. They zone areas for use for residential, commercial and other purposes and put restrictions in place. Restrictions could be anything from height limits to the colour buildings can be painted. Before you spend money on a planning application, find out from a planning officer what they would see as acceptable on the site you're looking at. If they think permission would be granted, consider sending in the application, but for *outline planning permission* to begin with. Outline planning permission is a way of testing the waters, so to speak – I guess a bit like getting a provisional driver's licence. You have permission but you haven't passed the detailed test. The benefit of applying for outline planning is twofold: the drawings needed are fairly basic and the application costs less than an application for full planning permission. If you get approval, you can then apply for full planning. You have three years to do so. You can get your architect to apply for you. They'll send in the correct drawings and deal with all the high-tech mumbo-jumbo. It'll save delays.

Tips

Knock on a door or two in an area you like. Someone may consider selling a site to you even though it wasn't up for sale. I know two people who got their sites this way.

Let the planning department of the council know you want to buy a site. They might know of a site that's just had planning approved and is going up for sale.

When you're viewing sites, bring a pad and paper with you, just like you would if you were buying a property. Take detailed notes and use your common sense.

Make sure you sweeten the locals. As part of the planning process, you have to give the public the right to object to your plans. An ad will have to be put in the newspaper and a *site notice* will have to be put up so that people have a chance to object to your plans.

Things To Do

Visit the local planning office to see if there are any restrictions for building in certain *zoned* areas. 'Zoned' is a term used to describe regulations for land – restrictions on building type, for example.

Check if only certain people can live in the area. Some county councils will only give planning to people who have lived in the area for a long time, who have family ties in the area or who work in the area. If you're a blow-in, you'll need to butter them up.

Check whether planning permission has been refused before and the reasons for the refusal. It could save you money and hassle.

Consider the surrounding areas and buildings. If you want to build a big funky house and the houses surrounding it are small cottages, planning would probably be refused. Having said that, I've seen some right eyesores pop their ugly heads up in cute little villages.

Consider whether the site suits your needs. If you need room for a pony, a small site would be pointless.

Where is the site positioned? If there's a steep slope nearby, you should think about a possible landslide. If the site is on top of a hill it may be very exposed and get a beating from harsh winds. If it's boggy, you could expect the foundations to cost a lot.

Consider the amount of preparation involved. Will the site need to be levelled or is there an existing building that will need to come down?

The subsoil structure should be looked at. The land may have been used as a smelly dump and could be contaminated, or old foundations may be hiding underneath. The council heritage department will be able to give you the low-down on what has been in the area.

What is the soil itself like? Not all soil types hold septic tanks, for example.

Is the site rocky or swamped? This might affect the septic tank or the water supply.

Is the site big enough to set back the house (from the road, for instance) if you're asked to?

What's the story with traffic? Would an access road interfere with the existing roads?

How easy is it to get a phone connection?

How easy is it to get an electricity supply?

Is there mobile-phone coverage?

Site Valuation

You need to have the site valued to make sure it's a good buy. The lender will ask you to do this before they give you a mortgage, the same as for a property mortgage. Check sites in the area to see if the asking price is fair. Don't buy just because a site is cheap. Look for quality and value for money.

Bricks and Mortar or Timber-frame?

In Ireland, the majority of properties are made from bricks and mortar, but timber-framed houses have really been showing their faces in the last few years. There are a number of reasons for this. Firstly, they offer quicker building times – about two to three months less than for brick buildings. They usually come in kit form and are easier to insulate than brick properties, and there isn't the long drying-out period that's required for brick properties. Secondly, the design of the property can often be downloaded from a computer and customised to your needs. And thirdly, pretty much any style of property can be copied, to the point where you wouldn't even know the house was timber-framed. So before you go ahead with a building project, consider all your options.

Finance

A mortgage for a site or a self-build is different from that on an existing property. Although the lender will ask the same questions regarding your ability to repay, the mortgage is set up differently. Rather than being drawn down in one lump sum, it's given in stages as needed. The advantage is that you often only have to pay interest on what's drawn down, so this eases financial stress. The bank take into account what the property will be worth when it has been completed. It's generally a pretty good increase, so they're usually fine with self-build mortgages.

To maximise your chances of getting the mortgage, choose a site with planning in place and put a proposal package together. Include the following:

Proof of ID

Utility bills as proof of address

Accounts (including loans outstanding)

Irish Credit Bureau (ICB) certificate confirming good credit history The ICB is a database of information detailing your repayment performance on loans and credit cards. Over forty financial institutions are registered with the ICB. If you apply for a loan, a lender will use the system to check you out. They want to know if you actually pay what you agree to pay. Your information is held on the database for five years after a credit agreement has been closed.

An accurate property plan drawn up by a qualified architect

A quantity surveyor's report outlining expected building costs

Builder's details

Planning permission certificate

Estimating Costs

You should always budget before taking on *any* project. Fill in the template below to help you.

Site cost:

Planning fees:

Building cost:

Foundations:

Place to live while property is being built:

Electrics and plumbing:

Windows:

Woodwork:

Basic furnishings (kitchen units, bathroom suite, etc):

Detailed furnishings (flooring, furniture):

Outside works (walls, paths, roads, etc):

Insurance fee:

Contingency fund (recommended 20 percent of the total estimated building cost):

Legal fees:

Architect and project management fees:

Mortgage payments:

Tips

The planning and design process can take a long time, so *an hourly rate can be expensive*. Have a written payment agreement in place before anyone does work.

Expect the project to take longer than the builders say. But make sure that the contract states that there'll be a penalty for any work not completed on time.

Overestimate the cost of the project. Unexpected extras always have a way of showing up. For a list of tradesmen and building resources in your area, visit *www.donnakennedy.com*.

The Engineer

The engineer will get the ball rolling. He or she will mark out the site boundaries so they can be put on an *Ordnance Survey map* (a map of the surrounding area). Next, they'll dig a big hole in the ground (a *trial hole*) to check whether the site is prone to floods. When that has been done, a site plan is drawn up to show where the house is positioned on the site, e.g. how close it is to the septic tank, the road and the water supply, and so on.

The Architect

Although you can design a property yourself, get a plan out of a book or buy one on the internet, using a qualified architect to design your property is advisable. They will draw up plans and elevations (maybe something really funky) and handle all the finicky bits with planning, etc. Find an architect who designs well, preferably one who has been recommended to you. If you don't have a recommendation, you could call the Royal Institute of Architects and they'll get you someone. Getting an architect can cost a bit, but all things considered, they're likely to save you money in the long run. Some charge a flat fee (often a proportion – typically 20 percent – of the overall cost of the project) and others by the hour. Check it out, and make sure you can accommodate it within your budget before taking someone on.

The Quantity Surveyor

It's important you know the step-by-step process involved in the project. The quantity surveyor should be able to tell you once they've looked at the project details. They'll give you an estimate on how much the project is likely to cost you, how long it will take to complete, who should do what, and when they should do it. If you employ an architect, they might do this job for you.

The Project Manager

A project manager is basically a site foreman, and if he or she is good, they're worth their weight in gold. The idea is for them to deal with the whole shebang from start to finish, making sure everything is done on time and in the right way. Sometimes an individual can take on the role of project manager, but normally it's the boss of the building firm who does it. Either way, the person you choose must know enough about construction to handle any problems that might occur. They'll be involved at every stage, so it's essential to have one.

The Builders

When you're building a single property, it's the norm to get a small company to do it – a local brickie, most likely. Big contractors are used for projects like housing estates. Before employing someone, get written quotations from at least three builders and compare what you're being offered with what it will cost. Check that the prices are realistic and find out if the quotations are estimated prices or fixed quotes, and if they include VAT. Check out the builder's reputation and ask to see some of their previous projects. They should be good. If you decide to go with a builder, make sure you get your solicitor to look at the details of the contract, especially the bit about payment terms and the timescale for the project.

The Builder's Job

The main contractor should be easygoing. They should provide good labour (sticking to regulations, getting insurance, and so on) and look after the running of the site (making sure there's a loo, etc) from start to finish. However, always check in with them on site to make sure the job is being done. Don't harass them, just keep an eye on them. And get a guarantee against faults. A ten-year guarantee is common.

Direct Labour

I don't recommend using direct labour (employing individuals to do work) first time around. It takes a heck of a lot of management and organisation. Even though direct labour can sometimes work out cheaper, it's generally not worth the hassle. Unless the tradesmen are reliable, expect to hear things like: 'Sorry, I can't make it today. I'm sick' . . . 'My granny died' . . . 'My car broke down' – when really they were out on the lash the night before and couldn't be bothered getting out of bed. But if you insist on going the direct-labour route, only employ people you know or people who have been recommended. State the terms clearly and in writing from the start. These would include:

Payment terms and conditions. Never pay for a job until it's finished.

Builder's insurance. Check the policy and what it covers. Don't put yourself in a situation where you could be liable for their negligence. You should also get insurance yourself.

A work schedule.

Qualifications. People employed to install gas and electrics should be part of a professional body.

Tip

Make sure the electrician embeds wiring into the wall. Some leave it sticking out (surface trunking) and it looks awful. It can take away from the value of the property and, once done, is expensive to change.

Problems

This is where you might need to get the boxing gloves out. Just kidding. What you will need is the ability to communicate what you want without getting people's backs up. You need to be assertive, especially if you're young. Even though you might have a project manager to deal with problems, when push comes to shove, there'll always be something you'll have to deal with yourself. To sort the problem out quickly, use a bit of psychology. Develop a rapport with whoever is causing the problem. Make them feel that you're on the same wavelength. You've got to be friendly. This is how I dealt with one particular problem. Just before the building was complete, I needed something fixed. I knew the foreman had already been harassed for this, that and the other by other people, so if I called him, he would probably fob me off or get angry. The thing was, if I didn't call him, the problem wouldn't be fixed. So what do you think I said to him? In a friendly tone: 'I can imagine you're sick of people calling you, and I know your time is valuable. But I have a problem with X and I feel you're the only person professional enough to deal with it. I would be so grateful if you would help me.' Now, what does that imply? Well, first it says that I'm friendly and value his time. Second, that I understand his position. Third, it presupposes that if he doesn't sort out my problem, he isn't professional enough. Who wants to feel they're not a pro? But the clincher was that I made him feel good about sorting out my problem. I put the presupposition within a compliment. Did he sort out my problem? Absolutely! Did he sort out my grumpy neighbour's problem? Absolutely not. Show appreciation. This can be done by something as simple as sending a thank-you text.

5

Moving

Before we talk about the moving process itself, it's important to consider how you're going to make your rental lease expiration date coincide with the moving date. It's something a lot of people worry about. 'What if the landlord wants me out and I can't find a place to rent for a month or two? Will I have to sleep on a park bench?' Well, if your landlord is any way decent, you should have nothing to worry about. Talk to them. Let them know the situation. As long as you give them enough notice to get another tenant, they're likely to be OK about it. They might draw up a month-to-month lease, or if there is only a short time to moving day they might just keep the deposit you paid at the beginning. The main thing to do is to let them know what you're doing. Never spring anything on a landlord!

Moving House

Most people see moving house as one big drag. And I guess in some ways it can be. It takes a bit of time, and admittedly it's not the most exciting activity you could do in your day. But what if you were to look at it another way? What if you were to use it as an opportunity to tidy up your life, so to speak? You could turn the dread into excitement if you look at it in a useful way. I see moving house as a perfect time to de-clutter all the crap you hoarded over the years – the things you know very well are just dust collectors. But that's not the only way to look at moving. It could be an opportunity to make some cash. Believe it or not, there are plenty of people willing to pay for your junk at a car boot sale.

DIY or Pros?

The first thing you'll need to decide is whether to go the DIY route and move your things yourself or get some professionals in to do the job for you. Your decision is likely to be based on the distance to your new gaff and how much stuff you intend to take with you. If it's going to be a long haul, it might not be a bad idea to hire a removal firm. Although this will cost you, it could save you hassle and time. If it's a straightforward pack-and-go move to an area nearby, get a few friends to help you out. A free pint normally does the trick!

Removal Firms

You can find removal firms in the phone book but you should really only employ one that (a) has been recommended to you or (b) has a longstanding reputation. The whole point of getting professionals in is to make your life easier. You need to be able to trust them. They should be able to provide references and have their own insurance, and their fees should be reasonable. The cost usually depends on the level of service you want. Most firms offer removal options. For example, load and unload only, full packing and load with unpacking, or packing and load with no unpacking. You could expect travel distance and petrol cost to influence the price as well. Get quotes from more than one company (get the price including VAT) and ask if they charge a flat fee or an hourly rate. If they're the type of guys who stop for a hundred cups of tea and fags on the job, an hourly rate would cost a bomb.

Tips

Make sure the firm has insurance for both your belongings and their staff. Check the small print to see what is and isn't covered under the policy.

Move your valuables yourself. You can't be sure one of the guys isn't a klutz.

Start Early

Unless you're a glutton for punishment, start packing well before the move date – a few weeks before, at least. Make it simple. Keep the following list handy and tick things off as you go along.

A Month Before

Arrange that the lease expiration date coincides with the moving day and ask for your deposit back if applicable.

Hire a removal firm or arrange transport with friends. Try to avoid moving on a weekday, during peak hours or on holidays. Traffic could get messy and if the firm charges an hourly rate you could end up with a nasty hole in your pocket. Parking might also be a problem.

Check with the local council if there are parking restrictions at your new address. If there are, you will need to arrange for the restrictions to be lifted for the move day.

Arrange storage if your home isn't going to be ready for the move date. A lot of removal firms can provide storage at a charge, but it's essential that your belongings are fully insured.

Arrange a sitter for children and pets.

Let your children's school know the move date.

Cancel services like bin collection and arrange them for your new address.

Make sure you have insurance for your new home. Get quotes. There is a huge variation among insurance policies, so compare what's on offer to get the best deal.

Make copies of all important documents like birth certificates, marriage certificates, death certificates, school records, employment documents, medical records, bank details and receipts for valuables.

Start de-cluttering. Sort out cupboards, the garage, the shed and the attic, and look out for upcoming car boot sales so you can flog unwanted junk.

Use up frozen food so the freezer can be defrosted.

Three Weeks Before

Get packing materials. Although you can buy bubble wrap and boxes, to keep costs down just take a trip to the supermarket and ask for their old cardboard boxes and newspapers. They'll be more than happy to give them to you; it saves them having to recycle. Use the newspaper to wrap your things in instead of paying for bubble wrap.

Buy some packing tape and a red marker pen to label boxes. If you don't label the boxes, be prepared for disaster.

If you're using a removal firm, make out an inventory of everything you pack. You can't be sure, no matter how reputable the company is, that the removal guys don't have sticky fingers! If you have an inventory that they sign, there won't be a problem.

Start packing anything you won't need for the next couple of weeks. Wrap everything carefully, and put things in labelled boxes. Some things (such as books) weigh a lot, so make sure they're in the bottom of the box and that when the box is full it can be lifted easily.

Write on the front of each box the room it should go in and put the word FRAGILE (in red) on boxes that contain breakable items. Write this on all sides of the box.

Back up any computer data and label all files. Box them together.

Leave packing anything flammable until a day or two before the move. Removal firms normally aren't insured to carry them, so you will have to move them yourself.

Two Weeks Before

Contact your bank, credit union and building societies to switch direct debits and standing orders to the new address at the right time.

Contact insurance companies (health, travel and car) and store-card companies. Give them your new address.

Contact electricity, gas and water supply companies to have meters read and to give them your new address.

Contact service providers for cable TV, internet and phone (both fixed and mobile).

Contact your GP, and if you're moving to a new area, have your records transferred.

Pack clothes and other belongings that you won't need for the next couple of weeks.

One Week Before

Contact the post office to have your mail redirected once you move. The charge will vary depending on how long you want the re-directing service to last.

Contact book, sports and social clubs.

Clean. A lot of people just up and leave, but it's downright rude. Besides, your contract might state that you have to leave the property the way you got it. That could mean repainting if you put bright colours on the walls while you were there.

Give friends and relatives your new address.

Return library books and rented DVDs.

Collect dry cleaning.

Arrange to pick up your keys from the estate agent or solicitor.

Tip

Leave out a few cups, plates, a kettle, cutlery and a radio/CD player. You'll want them the day you move in!

The Day Before

Check that everything is going according to plan with your solicitor and estate agent.

Give the removal company clear written instructions for the move. Provide a map with your new address highlighted on it and write your phone number on top of the map.

Draw up a list of numbers for tradesmen at your new address. Something might go wrong shortly after you move in: there might be a problem with the plumbing or the gas.

Go through each room to make sure everything has been packed.

Empty bins.

Charge your mobile phone. You need to be contactable.

Have a good snooze.

Moving Day

Eat a big breakfast. It might be a while before you eat again!

Go over instructions with the removal firm again. Make sure they have your phone number and another one in case they can't reach you.

Drop children and pets off at their sitters.

Get some biscuits, some other grub and tea/coffee on the way back. You might get hungry later in the day.

Check that you have your wallet, credit cards, chequebooks, driving licence, car keys and house keys.

Bring a phone directory, the vendor's contact details and the utility company's contact details.

Get supplies: light bulbs, plugs, tool kit, torch, loo roll, candles (in case of a blackout), cleaning products, vacuum cleaner, a brush, mop and baby supplies.

Say your farewells.

Your New Home

Arrive before the removal men or friends and make sure carpets are well protected from any muddy boots.

Ensure all *your belongings are put in the right rooms.*

Check the inventory so you know everything has arrived safe and sound.

Sign the inventory but remember to get your keys from the removal guys.

Have the kids and pets picked up and settle them in.

Have a well-deserved break.

Have a bit of a clean. It's easier to clean when there aren't things to trip over.

Have another break.

Tips

Arrange your insurance before *you move your stuff* just in case the boxes go walkabout.

Never move in your belongings unless you're moving in with them. Thieves are renowned for fleecing newcomers' properties. They linger on the day to see if you're moving in. If you're not, they'll wait until you're gone and have a whale of a time in your absence.

Never move your stuff at night or when it's dark. Safety first.

Don't allow people into your house until you get to know them, even if they say they're the gas man.

Don't leave the keys in the van or leave boxes outside, again in case of lingering brats.

Other Things To Do

Get instructions for using the gas, water, phone and electrics and check they work.

Locate the fuse box, gas mains and water stop tap in case of an emergency.

Make sure the security alarm, outside light and door/window locks work.

Have the electricity and gas meters read and contact the relevant companies.

Get the house sale sign removed. Thieving brats prey on new homeowners. There's a lot of new gear to swipe.

Test smoke alarms.

Test appliances.

Get a TV licence from the post office. I forgot about that one and freaked when the guy arrived at my door looking for it.

A Few Days After Moving In

It's important to get on with your neighbours, so pop around for some sugar kind-of-thing. Neighbours will help you settle in and keep an eye on your property when you're not there. Invite them to your house-warming.

The House-warming Party

Only one thing to say about this: have it before you decorate!

Problems

I have to say, had I not had a handy partner to sort out the heating systems, the boiler and all the rest, I would've been at a loss. And for all you sexists out there, no it's not because I'm a woman! It's because I didn't need to know how to sort out things like that before. Why would I? So if you happen to be like me and show a lack of enthusiasm for learning how to work house things, make sure you know someone who can help if you get stuck.

The Money Pinch

Running out of money in the early stages of home own-ership is something a lot of people worry about. My ad-vice is to buy what you can and save for the rest. Under no circumstances should you get out a loan to pay for furniture, no matter how tempted you are. That includes using credit cards. If you don't trust yourself not to shop, then cut up the cards. Spending when you can't af-ford to is like throwing yourself into a sea of sharks. What seems lovely and refreshing at the beginning can eat you up in a heartbeat. So always pay cash. Try to bor-row furniture from relatives for the first while, and wait until the sales or check out the *Buy & Sell*. And you don't have to go all-out on the décor either. There's plenty you can do to make your property look good on a tight budget. Here are a few ideas.

Decorating: Makeover Magic

The first thing you need to do is blitz the place, one room at a time. Take down curtains and blinds and take out whatever furniture is in the room. Clear out the creepy-crawlies and brush away the cobwebs. When the room is like a blank canvas, it's easy to imagine the new look.

Flooring

Does the existing carpet or lino (nasty!) need to be ripped up? If it's one of those swirly sixties ones, the answer is yes. If you can't afford to change it, consider covering it up with a large rug and choose something neutral so that patterns and colours don't clash. If it's a wooden floor, think about sanding it and either varnishing or painting it (in a dark colour). If you can spruce it up, don't bother changing the floor covering. When you get some spare money, you can change it. Prioritise what needs to be done in the house and what will have maximum effect for minimum cost.

Walls

Check out the walls. If they're papered, you don't necessarily have to take the paper off. This takes a bit of work, and if you need to get it steamed it can cost a bit too. So if your budget is squeezed and you don't like the wallpaper, see if you could get away with painting over it. If the walls aren't papered, you could use sugar soap to get rid of any grubby marks, or paint the room a new colour. Changing the colour of a room is the easiest way to update it, so becoming colour-conscious is essential to a good makeover. For example, painting a room in a neutral colour or a pastel colour has an opening-up effect. It makes the room feel brighter and bigger. You could paint the same room in a dark shade and, unless the room is very big to start off with, it could end up feeling like a small cave. To get the best look, choose a pale background colour and add an accent colour (a strong colour) in a smaller area to create impact. Accent colours are used to make a feature area and can be reflected in accessories in the room. In the living room, the fireplace is often the feature area, with the chimney breast or either side of it being painted another colour. You can use accent colours to shorten, widen or lengthen a room too. To make it feel shorter or wider, paint the narrow walls at either end of the room a strong colour and use horizontal lines. This could be done by laying the floorboards pointing across the room as opposed to lengthways, or by using a horizontal line in the paint or wallpaper design. On the other hand, if you want to make a room look longer, paint the longer walls in the accent colour and point any horizontal stripes towards the narrow walls. You can also play around with the ceiling: painting it a slightly darker shade than the walls gives the impression of lowering it.

Tips

Look for bargains in paint stores. Big outlets have offers on all the time, so scout them out. White paint is usually cheaper, so to keep costs down you could go for a white background and get a more expensive-looking accent colour.

Satin or matt accent colours tend to look nicer than gloss. Gloss shows dust.

If you're buying a new house, get the builders to tack on the skirting boards rather than fixing them. It'll make it easier to paint the walls and save you having to drag them off if a floor is to be laid.

Paint dust sealer on new concrete floors so rising dust doesn't ruin paintwork.

If rooms are small or dark, put up large mirrors. You can get cheap-framed mirrors that you can tart up by either changing the frame or painting it.

Choosing the Right Colour

It's important to choose colours you like, but they should also compliment the room. Apart from having an opening-up or closing-in effect, different colours create different atmospheres in a room. Before choosing colours, sit down and decide on the effect you want to create. Do you want the room to feel chilled-out or energetic, peaceful or stimulating? To help you decide, here's a list of colours and the effect they can have.

Green

Green is a colour associated with nature. It's calming and gives a sense of security and stability. Use it in bedrooms, living rooms and hallways. Try not to use green with a blue tinge: it can be very cold.

Red

Red is associated with passion, adventure, energy and warmth. It works well in dining rooms. It promotes sociable feelings and stimulates appetite but don't overdo it. It can easily become overpowering, so you might like to use a toned-down version.

Orange

Orange is a warm colour linked to stability, security and good digestion. It's good for living rooms and dining rooms.

Blue

Blue is perfect for those whose pastime is looking at fluffy-cloud rabbits and trains in the sky. It is calming and soothing and promotes intellectual thought. Use it in studies, bathrooms and possibly in the bedroom, as long as it's a blue with a warm undertone. Pale blue can be a bit North Pole-like.

White

White can look great in pretty much every room but you have to be really careful about the shade of white you choose. To the ordinary individual, white is white, but there are subtle differences. If you paint a room white and the paint has a blue tinge to it, expect to feel like you're in a dental surgery or a hospital: it will feel sterile and cold. On the other hand, if you paint a room white with a warm undertone, it gives a really fresh and spacious feel, and you won't need to worry about matching up furniture, as you might in a room painted in a richer colour. If you feel that white is a bit bland, give it a bit of oomph by using bright accessories.

Pink

Pink can create anything from lovey-dovey feelings to girly-wirly ones. Hot fuchsia stimulates passion, so it's good for master bedrooms, but it should be used sparingly. Pastel pink, on the other hand, induces restful feelings, and you don't have to be so skimpy with it. But I don't recommend that you use it in the master bedroom: it's too princessy.

Yellow

Yellow is a happy-clappy colour. It's an energetic, feel-good colour and is perfect for kitchens and north-facing rooms.

Purple

Purple is for creativity, joy and hanky-panky. Use in bedrooms.

Brown

An au-natural colour that goes with pretty much anything. Toned-down browns are good. Pair them with cream, gold, green or blue to get a classy look. Chocolate, mocha and cream are especially nice together.

Black

Black is good as an accent colour or when used in accessories, but never use it as an all-over colour. It's depressing and gives off that 'It's so unfair' teenage vibe.

Furnishings

Furniture is something that a lot of first-time buyers simply don't have. Have a scout around the property to see if the seller left anything stylish that you could use; things like nice curtains, blinds (recommended for small rooms to maximise space) or light fittings. If you washed them, how would they look? Could you add something to them to make them look funkier: a tab or pelmet on a plain curtain or blind that blends with your colour scheme, for example? The item might even suit another room, so keep that in mind. Think about where you place furniture in the room. If you have a piece you really like, show it off. Make it the feature area. Don't put too much or too little in a room. Keep it balanced.

The Living Room

If you have a couch and it's a bit ropey, consider putting a nice throw on it until you can afford a new one. Or get washable slipcovers and blend them with the accent colour on the walls. Plain colours, neutrals and stripes work best on furniture coverings. Alternatively, you might consider buying a sofa bed. It will double up as a bed if you don't have one. When you can afford a proper bed, the sofa will always be there as a spare for guests.

Think about existing fitted furniture. You might get away with just cleaning it up, painting it or varnishing it. Keep the colour similar to the walls, or maybe a shade darker, so it isn't an eyesore.

What about the fireplace? Replacing it can be expensive, so if you don't like it you can distract attention away from it by creating a feature area in another part of the room, or you could jazz it up. Clean it and put a cluster of candles or a vase of flowers on the hearth. Try to pick up the accent colour in the room.

Look at the light fitting. If it's dodgy, you can buy something that looks better for next to nothing. Take a trip to the bargain stores for this one. End-of-the-line stock can be a life-saver.

The Bathroom

The shower and bath should be clean, so take off any grubby stains. Bleach might be enough to do it.

If the shower curtain is a bit grim, replace it with something new and simple. White is best, maybe with a small pattern.

Cover up a grubby floor with a big twist-towelling bath mat.

If the tiles are dated or broken, ideally replace them. But if you can't re-tile, clean up dirty-looking grout with a grout pen – a chunky pen that dispenses a thin layer of white grout. It'll immediately make them look newer. Another option is tile paint.

If the bathroom isn't tiled but the area around the bath looks bad, simply paint it with a waterproof paint until you can afford tiles.

If the bathroom is small, tile halfway up walls in a pale colour. Consider tiling the side of the bath with the same tiles. It gives an expensive look.

Think about changing the taps. Depending on where you get them, the price can be fairly good, and they make a huge difference to the overall look. The cheaper option is to doll up the chrome using descaler; even cheaper again, vinegar in water will banish limescale.

A mirror will make a statement and create a feeling of space. You can get one for a pittance – or free if you ask a glazier for a polished offcut.

Nice baskets or boxes could be used instead of a toiletry cabinet.

A blind could be replaced by no blind! Obviously this would only apply if you weren't overlooked.

Use candles, shells and coloured towels as accessories, either on the window, on a shelf or around the bath.

The Kitchen

It's easy to improve a kitchen on a low budget. Here are a few tips:

Paint the walls a neutral colour to maximise light.

Replace the door handles on the units to change the look instantly. Plain brushed-stainless-steel handles look really good.

Think about painting the unit doors rather than getting a new kitchen.

Ask a kitchen maker if they'll sell you a work surface at a good price.

Improve a rough-looking table with a trendy tablecloth. It could blend with the blinds or curtains. If you're not handy with a sewing machine, find someone who is and ask them to make you some cushions and seat slips. To cut costs, get offcuts from a material store.

The Bedroom

Apart from a paint job, the easiest way to improve a bedroom is to use nice bed linen, place cushions neatly and keep the room clutter-free. Nice bedside lamps go a long way too. You can get them at a good price easily enough.

So you see, you never have to live in a place that isn't nice. Just start small and try to improve it as you go along.

* * *

So what happens after you move in? Well, for some people that's pretty much it. The dream of owning their own gaff has been realised, and they're happy campers. But if you're wise, you might decide to use the property to make you rich! Now before your brain starts working overtime, I understand that when you're buying your first property, making money from it is probably the last thing on your mind. You just want the keys. And initially it was that way for me too – until I realised that I could be depriving myself, that is. I invite you now to read the following information.

6

Adding Value

Always add value to any property you buy. This puts you in a great financial position if you decide to invest in more property. (We'll discuss this in more detail later on.) All too often, the phrase 'add value' involves clueless property hopefuls, bulldozers, collapsing roofs and bursting pipes – basically people who don't know what 'add value' means. Having looked at a property programme or two, they bulldoze the walls and get too excited about making the property *nice*. Making a property nice does not necessarily add value to it. All it does is make *you* like it more. Not everyone has the same taste or desires as you. You have to have a solid plan to make this work. The plan should be detailed and specific.

Questions To Ask

How, specifically, do I want to add value, and which rooms will I concentrate on?

How long will the project take to complete?

Will I have to take time off work during the project? How much will it cost me?

Will I need alternative accommodation during the project?

How much will I need to spend on the project? A quantity surveyor will give you an estimate.

If I am to make a profit from the project, what is the maximum I can spend?

Will I manage the project or will I get a professional to do this?

Who do I need to have on board for the project? Architect, surveyor, solicitor, tradesmen and so on.

What materials will I need, and where can I get them? How much will they cost?

What is my schedule of works for the property?

Are the tradesmen available at their planned slots? Be realistic by allowing extra time in the schedule.

When you're drawing up your plan, be realistic, allowing for weather and time delays relating to personal circumstances. For a list of tradesmen and building resources in your area, visit *www.donnakennedy.com.*

Specific Ways To Add Value

Extend

Think practical and think quality. An extension can bump up the value of a property no end, but only if it's done properly. There's no point in sticking a big blob on the back of your property just to make the house bigger. In fact, it could potentially reduce the value of the property. Take note of the following:

The extension should suit the property and should blend in with the surrounding area.

Check with your planning office to make sure it's OK to build the extension. If it doesn't take up more than three-quarters of the garden, it should be fine.

The extension shouldn't swallow up the garden. If your property is on a residential estate where there are families, take it that if you decide to sell on later, a person with a family will be the likely buyer. Nobody wants their children to play in a concrete box.

Only add a room that makes sense. There's no point adding a room just for the sake of it. If the house would benefit from an extra bedroom, an office or a bigger kitchen, that might be something to think about. Adding things like a snooker room won't add value, no matter how cool you think it is.

Consider the foundation. If it's a single-storey extension, the foundation is pretty basic. If you're extending upwards, the foundation will need to be able to hold the weight.

Install central heating and double-glazed windows. This applies to the rest of the property as well.

Make sure the electrics and plumbing are fitted properly and that everything is regulated.

Tips

Get a professional to dig a small hole next to the property to expose the foundations. If the house needs underpinning, it could cost a lot of money.

If you want to sell a property, get planning for an extension even if you don't intend to build one. It will make the property more attractive to buyers.

Converting the Attic

An attic is a hidden gem. It's tucked away, just crying out for attention. Have a snoop around to see what you might be able to do with it. There are a few things to consider for a conversion, but in the grand scheme of things it's crazy not to cash in on it. Again, only do what will put money *in* your pocket.

What rooms would the property benefit from having? An extra en-suite bedroom or study is often the best bet.

How much are you willing to spend? Factor in a contingency fund for the unexpected but stick to your budget. Spend on the space that will be lived in most.

Look at the shape of the roof. This will determine the design and layout of the room (or rooms).

Use the space well. The space running along the length of the house could be used for storage, possibly wardrobes.

Consider room size. Don't try to cram in more rooms thinking that this will add value. Squishy rooms are awful. From floor to ceiling should measure at least eight foot, and the floor area should be able to hold a single bed with room to move around.

Look at the supporting beams and joists. They need to be able to hold the weight of a floor and whatever will be on the floor (furniture and so on). They can be strengthened, but consider the cost involved.

Consider the heating. The existing boiler may not be able to feed the extra radiators needed. The cost of replacing them could be steep. To solve the problem, think about installing a small unvented electric boiler.

Try to fix radiators to internal walls. A radiator on an external wall is less efficient.

Fit a proper stairs that doesn't look like it just fell out of the sky. It should look like it's meant to be there. A windy stairs might be a good idea if space is tight but make sure you can get furniture up it.

Good insulation is a must, but not just for heat. The floor needs to be soundproofed if you don't want people screaming at you about your loud music. Soundproofing is fairly straightforward if you lay a heavy mineral-fibre quilt between the joists.

Tips

Make sure you get your builder to (a) sign a building contract and (b) get his own insurance. Cover yourself against the cowboys.

If the house is semi-detached, tell the neighbours what you're doing.

Design

The windows you fit should look good and be big enough to get out of in case of fire. Skylight Velux windows are the most common, probably because they're neat and in most cases you don't need planning permission for them, at least if they're at the back of the house. But if the windows are intended for the front of the house, especially if they're dormer-style, you might need approval. Make sure to check it out before you make any holes in the roof.

Fit plug sockets where they will be needed. They should suit the room layout. Fit at least two socket points per room and at least one in the hall.

Take radiators into account when you're designing the layout of a room. It's amazing how often people forget about them.

Put in a fire escape. If possible, stay away from anything big and ugly.

Converting the Garage

This is an easy way to add another room to the house. The main things to consider are lining exterior walls, installing heating (preferably oil or gas) and putting in a separate electrical circuit for power sockets and lights.

Period Pieces

If there's anything original (like cornicing, sash windows, wood beams, or cast-iron or marble fireplaces) that match the period of the house, keep them. If a previous owner ripped them out and put in naff alternatives, try to reclaim the original or something close to it.

Specific Rooms

Adding value means focusing on the right places. There are two rooms you should concentrate on: the kitchen and the bathroom. The other rooms are secondary, and a paint job is often enough to give them a facelift. A good kitchen and bathroom can add an average of €10,000 to a house, but you won't be spending that much to do it up. If you do it the clever way, you should get away with a few thousand euro.

The Kitchen

The kitchen probably adds the most value to a property. Think spacious, simple, clean and fashionable.

The kitchen units should be in good condition and should be in keeping with the property. If the units are bad, change them. You don't need to knock out the old units; you could just change the doors and handles to modern ones and fit a new worktop. If the units are really bad, and changing the doors won't cut it, you can get a decent-looking flat-pack kitchen from wholesale or large outlet stores quite cheaply. If your market is at the upper end of the scale, make sure to put in a designer-look kitchen. It may be more expensive but it's worth it.

The room should be bright and airy. There's nothing worse than a pokey, dark kitchen. If you need to knock through a wall to make the kitchen bigger (bigger kitchens add value), do, as long as this doesn't detract from the rest of the house. There should be enough room for a table and chairs.

Flooring should be clean and practical. Tile the floor if you can, or at least get decent lino with a tile effect.

Accentuate features. For example, an Aga in a country kitchen will add value. And you can get good ones second-hand. The price of a new one won't justify the cash return. If you can pick up a Belfast sink cheaply, do, and get it fitted.

In apartments, keep things streamlined. Think trendy and sleek. Business professionals go for apartments, so consider their lifestyle. They like to entertain, so the kitchen/dining room is their area of interest.

Make sure there's enough storage space. Add a utility room next to the kitchen if there's room.

The Bathroom

The bathroom is the second most used room in the house, so it's worth giving it some attention. You can add value here cheaply.

Make sure the layout is practical. Squashing a shower into a tiny space won't do. You need to be able to get in and out of it.

Replace coloured suites with white ones. You can get them for a few hundred euro nowadays.

Tile the floors (with non-slip tiles). Carpet stinks after getting wet, and lino lifts off the floor.

Fit a shower and, if there's room and the property will benefit from having one, fit a bath. People want a shower but they like to have options, especially families.

Update with new taps. They can be got really cheaply but make a huge difference.

En-suite Bathrooms

People expect en-suites, at least in the master bedroom, so if there's room and it's within budget, have one fitted.

Tip

Buy tiles, flooring, fittings and fixtures in the sales or from a wholesaler. It will save you loads. A lot of places will allow you to pick out what you want, and after you place a deposit on whatever it is you're buying, you can pay it off over a few months. This is worth doing if you don't have the money upfront.

Other Areas

Garden

A garden should look inviting but not fussy. So no ugly gnomes! The key to adding value with a garden is keeping it simple, stylish and easy to maintain. If you plant flowers everywhere, it means that the buyer has to work hard to maintain the look. I recommend that you divide the garden into sections. You might have a lawn area (especially for a family), a rockery and a planted area, but nothing fussy. Use plants that are hardy and don't need much work. Plants like heathers, ferns, grasses and evergreens look good every time. Alternatively, you could just pea-shingle the area and put some trendy pots on display.

Patio

A patio doesn't have to be expensive and can be a good feature. Use decking or stone for the ground surface. To make the patio look inviting, place plants in a few simple decorative pots at different heights. Think outdoor chill-out room.

Grants

In specific cases, and in certain areas, loans are available from the council for improving or extending your property.

Disabled Person's Grant

This grant covers the cost of adapting a private home for a person with a disability (discussed in more detail in Chapter 2).

Thatching Grant

This is to cover the cost of repairing or renewing thatched roofs.

Mortgage Subsidy

This subsidy is available for a local-authority tenant who wants to give up their home to buy a property on the open market. Financial help may be given for up to five years.

Housing Aid for Older People Scheme

The Scheme of Housing Aid for Older People is available to assist older people who are living in poor housing conditions to have necessary repairs or improvements carried out. The effective maximum grant under this scheme is €10,500, which may cover up to 100 percent of the cost of works.

You can get more information about grants from your local authority or the Department of the Environment, in Ballina, County Mayo (1890 305030).

7

Investing in the Property

For years, we've seen people become extremely wealthy through property investing. But with this whole recession business, isn't it time that investors finally hung up their hats? Shouldn't they just come to the same conclusion as everyone else: that you can't make money from property any more. Well – no.

Investors are wealthy because they don't take recessions lying down. They use what they know, and play the market to their advantage. They do not give in to others' fears or negative thinking. They use what they have and reap the rewards. And once *you* own a property, you can too.

Realistically, you're not going to make a fortune from property in the next couple of years. However, the principles of making money from property still hold true, and history shows that property markets eventually come good again. So if you take a medium- to long-term view of things and do the groundwork now, you'll be happy in a few years' time.

So let's look at how property investors do it.

Releasing Equity from the Property You Already Have

Equity release (sometimes called a *top-up mortgage*) is the way investors climb the property ladder without using their own money, and it's essential to understand how it works. I found the concept hard to understand when I started, so I'm going to explain it the easy way, by using an example.

Steps

1. You buy a property (your home) for €300,000. For this example, we'll assume that you've taken out a 90 percent mortgage on it (€270,000).

2. After a year or two, having done a bit of work to the property (adding value), you get the property re-valued. It's now valued at €360,000. This means that you've created €60,000 of value within the property (Property value €360,000 – mortgage €300,000 = €60,000). This is known as *equity*.

3. You want to buy another property. You find one, say for €150,000.

4. You approach the bank for the money to buy the property. They agree to give you 70 percent of the money for the investment property (€105,000); you'll have to come up with the remaining 30 percent (€45,000). In theory, you don't have it. Or do you?

5. This is where that €60,000 equity comes in. You can use it (in a process known as *releasing equity*)

to finance the deposit on the investment property. The bank will allow you to top up your home mortgage (currently €270,000) to get the deposit for the buy-to-let. The new mortgage on your home will be €315,000. The mortgage on the investment property (the 80 percent agreed) is €105,000. And your tenant in the investment property will be paying that mortgage. All to come!

Tip

Make sure you reapply for tax relief when you top up your mortgage.

I don't suggest you take out 100 percent mortgages. Raise the deposit in other ways, as discussed in Chapter 2.

Tax-incentive Properties

Some investors, especially if they have a big property portfolio, buy tax-incentive properties. They still use the equity-release method but the properties chosen are bought within schemes.

Section 23

In the 1980s, the government decided that rental accommodation needed to improve. They came up with a scheme called Section 23. This scheme allows investors to buy certain properties, normally in run-down or rural areas, and claim tax relief on them. This is a great tax break for investors who have a good-sized property portfolio. Sometimes the apparent relief is sneakily factored into the price, though, so make sure you do your sums and only buy if the deal makes sense.

Section 50

This scheme involves student accommodation. Relief can also be claimed against the rental income. The properties have to be new and purpose-built, and located within a few miles of a college or university. Again, beware that the tax saving for section properties is often factored into the purchase price. Do your figures.

Tips

Get a good accountant. They'll help you take legal advantage of tax allowances. If they're good at their job, they'll know all the allowances, even the hush-hush ones.

To maximise monthly rental income from your investment, consider stretching mortgage repayments over a relatively long term. As an investor, this will be between twenty-five and thirty years. Although you end up paying more interest in the long run, if you intend to hold on to the property indefinitely (which you should if you want to make money), and given the fact that property prices generally double roughly every seven to ten years, does it matter how long the mortgage term is? Besides, you won't be paying the interest; your tenant will. Holding makes more sense to me. When a property is sold, a big lump of the profit goes to Mr Taxman, in the form of Capital Gains Tax (CGT). Why on earth would you give money to the taxman when you can keep the property and make money? Unless you're selling an investment property to pay off the mortgage on your own home (which you should do eventually) why sell? There's no sense in it.

Tip

Pay the capital and interest on your home mortgage but not on an investment property (buy-to-let) mortgage.

What To Buy

Before you go looking for a buy-to-let investment, you've got to sit down and think things through. Why do you want the property, and what do you want it to do for you? Do you want to receive rental income every month (*cash flow*, explained below) or do you hope for capital appreciation (also explained below)? Some people want money from the property every month, some people rely solely on capital appreciation (common with foreign investment, but I don't see this as being wonderful in Ireland over the next few years), and some people want cash flow *and* capital appreciation. Whatever you want, the property has to work for you, not the other way around. There's no point in buying a property just so you can tell your friends you have one, and end up in dire straits because of it.

Capital Appreciation

I don't see property prices increasing hugely in Ireland over the next few years, so I don't buy properties that I have to subsidise every month. Instead, I buy under-market-value properties, and add value, or *force apprecia-tion*, as it is often called. This gives immediate equity, so I can fund another deal. You might ask why anyone would sell a property for less than it's worth. The simple answer is: who cares! If they're willing to sell and it's a worthwhile property, don't analyse! It's not up to you to point out the value in their property. It's up to you to spot the value and take advantage of it.

Cash Flow

When I buy a property, I make sure that it will put money in my pocket every month as it increases in value. This is called generating cash flow. It refers to the money left over from the rent you receive every month after the mortgage payment has been paid. And despite what people tell you, it is possible to generate cash flow in any market. You just need to buy the right properties. I don't recommend that you buy anything that won't give you cash flow. Unless you're sure the property will increase substantially in value, don't subsidise a property with your own money. The deal has to make sense, and you have to come out on top.

Tip

Always charge rent by the week for maximum cash flow. Look at the following example to see why:

Monthly rent payment of €700 (assumes €175 a week)

Weekly rent payment of €175

€175 x 52 weeks (one year) = €9,100

€9100 ÷ 12 months = €758

People naturally assume that there are four weeks in a month, when in actual fact there aren't. By charging rent weekly, you end up getting the true value in the year. In this case, you gain €58 extra a month.

Tip

Remember to bid low on properties. The cheaper you get them, the more money you can make.

Yield

When buying a property, you should always calculate the *yield*. This is a measurement of the annual cash return expressed as a percentage. The higher the yield, the better the investment (presupposing that the property allows for appreciation). Personally, I don't buy anything unless it will give me a yield of at least 6 percent. Calculate the yield as follows:

$$\frac{\text{Yearly rent received} \times 100}{\text{Full mortgage owed on the property}} = \% \text{ yield}$$

Incorporate Stamp Duty

When you're working out what return you can expect from a property, you should account for your full mortgage, not just the price you bought the house for. Incorporate any paid stamp duty into the equation. Stamp duty is tax you have to pay to the government when you buy a property. The payment covers the change in documents to state that you are the new owner of the property. The amount due varies with the purchase price of the property.

Tips

Investors looking for positive cash flow often buy resale properties, not new ones. Resale properties usually offer better value for money.

One-bedroom apartments have the best rentals in cities. Larger houses rent better in the country and in suburbs.

Identify Your Market

It's important to identify and get to know your market inside and out. Will you be renting to professionals, families or students? The type of tenant you target will help determine the type of property you buy, and where you buy. You need to be specific about your market to ensure maximum occupancy. Professionals and couples wanting to live in a city tend to go for one- or two-bedroom apartments, so if that's your market, buy apartments. Families tend to prefer houses (although they don't need to be luxurious), so a three- or four-bed semi in a quiet estate would be your best bet. If you're going after the student market, you'll need to consider two things. Firstly, is the property within walking distance of the college? Students don't like walking too far after a night on the beer. Secondly, are you going to rent by the room or as a single unit? If you rent a property by the room and it's in a good rental area, a bigger property, maybe a four-bed, should give better returns than a three-bed. If you were to rent the house as a single unit, the extra bedroom or two won't be needed, so the higher property price couldn't be justified. You also need to consider the furnishing when you're buying an investment property. Furniture for family houses needs to be durable and dark in colour (because of children's sticky paw marks and so on). Business professionals in town are likely to want more stylish stuff. Students, on the other hand, don't need fancy furniture. A little tip for you: don't splash out on student accommodation. When I was at college, the guys in my house – and they were decent guys – burned one of the chairs so they could buy a pint rather than having to buy fuel!

Tip

Check the demand for the property. Look at property websites and monitor the rental accommodation in the area for a month or two. If the properties are being swiped up, demand is likely to be high.

Check the going rents in the area. Ask other landlords about their experience before you buy in that area.

You'll find that expensive properties may not deliver better returns just because they look nice. The same applies to larger properties. That's why investors tend to buy average-looking three-bed semis or one- to two-bed apartments. Weigh up the situation. Is the extra cost for an expensive or larger property worth it relative to the rents you could expect to receive? Remember, investing in property is business, not emotional attachment.

Location

Pay particular attention to up-and-coming areas. Look at town development plans in order to maximise the chances of capital appreciation. Look for areas with universities (this opens up the student market), large factories (employees need homes), commuter belts, good transport links, shops and nightlife.

Tip

Look out for skips. If people are improving their homes, this could be an indication that an area is in transition.

Look for a property with a twist. This could include:

    potential to extend to the side

    potential for a garage or attic conversion

    potential at the rear for a flat or studio

    potential to divide a property into separate apartments

Getting the Property Ready

Before you let your property out, it has to be habitable. You've been a renter, so you know the story about what's needed. You don't really need luxury, but you don't want drafty windows and dirty furniture. So the win-win situation is *comfortable but not luxurious.*

Standards

Legally, your property has to meet certain standards. This is what is generally required, but it's worth checking the Department of Environment website (*www. environ.ie/en/Legislation/DevelopmentandHousing*) for up-to-date information on the regulations:

Good property structure. You don't want to be responsible for an injury to one of your tenants.

Proper electricity and heating systems. These need to be checked now and again.

Good ventilation in rooms.

A toilet, a sink (with hot and cold water) and a bath or shower. Bathrooms can be shared with other flats as long as they're within a two-stairs distance of each other and there's at least one toilet, and a bath or shower, for every two flats.

Safe and clean common areas.

Safe stairs and handrail.

Working fire safety system, including smoke alarms, defined escape routes, fire extinguishers, fire blanket and fire doors. Get a fire safety guide (*Fire Safety in Flats*) from the Department of the Environment to get more information.

Insurance

Again, always get insurance. Remember to shop around and negotiate the rate.

Furnishing the Property

If you're going to furnish your property – which is pretty standard in Ireland but not in other countries – keep it simple. You're not going to be living in it, and you need to keep costs to a minimum. People like to put their own stamp on things anyway. Use the inventory below as a guide. Draw up an inventory specific to your property and get your tenants to sign it. If they break anything, you need proof that it existed and that it was in good shape when they moved in. Put in second-hand furniture or furniture that you can replace every few years. Discount stores and catalogue stuff is fine.

Tip

Look out for hotels renovating or selling up. They often sell furniture to the public because it means that they don't have to store it or pay to have it taken away. They usually sell it for next to nothing. I kitted out a full house with hotel furniture for €450!

The Kitchen

Decent kitchen units (changing the doors and handles may be enough to update it)

Blinds

Cooker

Fridge-freezer combined

Washing machine (a combined washer-dryer is an option, particularly if space is tight)

Microwave

Dining table and chairs

Vacuum cleaner

Mop, bucket, sweeping brush, and dustpan and brush

Ironing board and iron

Saucepans and frying pan

Kettle

Crockery and cutlery

Bin

The Living Room

Sofa and armchairs

Curtains or blinds

Coffee table

Side table

Lamp

TV/DVD (optional)

The Bedroom

Double or single bed (depends on room size)

New mattress with cover

Bedside lockers and reading lamps

Wardrobe

Chest of drawers

Curtains or blinds

The Bathroom

Shower and curtain/screen

Bathroom suite

Shelf

Storage cabinet

Towel rail

Toilet-roll holder

Toilet brush and holder

Mirror over sink

Bin

The Hallway

Hall table

Doormat

Tip

Always tailor the furniture to the tenant renting the property. Never put in new, expensive furniture if the tenant has children living with them.

8

Letting the Property

Agent or DIY?

Now that your property is ready to rock and roll, the question is: are you going to use an agent to do the letting/managing, or are you going to do it yourself? Your decision will depend on two things:

The number of properties you own. If you only have one, letting it yourself may not be a big deal. But if you have ten, doing the letting could become a full-time job.

How bothered you are about being woken up at 2 AM by a tenant looking for spare keys.

Letting Agents

If you decide to use an agent, employ one that lets *and* manages the property. A lot of agents will get a tenant for you but they won't manage the property. This defeats the purpose of getting an agent, if you ask me. If you don't want to go down the DIY route, you want to be able to avoid doing any of the work. The agent must offer a good service.

Choosing an Agent

The agent should be competent, experienced and fully licensed.

They should be able to handle difficult tenants.

Check how many properties they have on their books and how quickly they rent them. Good numbers indicate success.

The agent should be able to market the property. Ask them how they intend to market it and who they intend to let it to. You have the right to approve tenants.

Look at what the agent is offering you. Are they giving the best value for money? A cheaper agent is not necessarily a better option. Look for quality service.

The agent should prepare the tenancy agreement, collect and hold the deposit, pay bills and carry out inspections.

If the agent is managing the property, they should have reliable tradesmen on standby in case of emergency repairs.

Tips

Make sure the quote from the agent includes VAT. The fee for full management should not be more than 10 to 12 percent of the annual rental income.

Using an agent has tax advantages. You can claim back the tax on fees they charge for maintenance. If you maintain the property yourself, you can't.

Letting It Yourself

The Rent

Research the going rate for rents in the area and set your rent around that. As with any business, you need to be aware of your competition and be able to handle it. Trying to bump the rent up for the sake of getting more money could easily backfire on you. Firstly, potential tenants don't want to pay more than they have to. Secondly, if you get a tenant and charge them crazy rent, and they find out their neighbour is paying much less they won't be too happy. But once you've set your rent, don't be pushed to reduce it. A person who backs you into a corner and gets away with it is likely to chance doing it again. *Never* give the impression you're a submissive landlord. They'll take you for a ride if you do.

Getting a Tenant

To get a tenant, you could advertise in the local paper, on supermarket noticeboards and on property websites. If you intend to let to students, go to the college and tell the students' union you have a property to rent. Put ads on noticeboards with tear-off phone-number strips.

Interviewing Tenants

Always interview potential tenants. Don't be afraid to ask them questions, but do respect their privacy. Ask for references but beware that they may not be reliable. I know plenty of people who got friends to pose as referees. You can never tell if a referee is legit or not. For this reason, ask for a bank reference, to show a good record of rent payments. Only a lying genius could get out of that.

Questions to ask a potential tenant:

What do you do for a living?

Are you working in the area?

Have you rented before? Where?

Do you have children? What age are they? Young children can be messy.

Do you have pets? My father rented an apartment to a girl who had a dog. The dog wasn't let out very often, so he did his business on the carpet every day. Don't allow pets in apartments!

If the person is stumbling to answer questions, they may be hiding something.

Tips

Beware of really young guys arriving in suits. Unless they're into wearing their Sunday best, which the occasional guy is, chances are they're making themselves out to be something they're not. This is a student classic. They'll tell you on the phone they're professionals to get the room, but they ain't!

Check out the car. Pretentious, I know, but cars can be indicative of financial circumstances.

When a potential tenant arrives to view the property, always tell them that someone else is interested in it. Tell them that you won't be able to give them an answer as to whether they can rent the property until you speak to the other viewers. I learned to use this trick from a friend of mine who had trouble with tenants. He met them at the property, and the minute he saw them his brain went: 'These guys are trouble'. The problem was that he was too afraid to say no to them. He knew they would accuse him of all sorts, so he let them take the property.

Managing

If you get a decent tenant, management should be handy enough. Have the tenants pay the rent directly into your account.

House Rules

Agree at the outset that you'll visit the house every two months for an inspection, and give the tenant a set of written house rules to sign. House rules are to be given whether you're going DIY or through an agent. They include:

Put the rubbish out for collection on the right day.

Sanitary towels, wipes and other similar products are not to be put down the loo in case of blockage.

Cookers, fridges and carpets are to be cleaned regularly.

The property in general should be kept clean inside and out.

Parking is only allowed in designated areas.

Noise levels need to be kept to a minimum (so you don't upset Nancy in No. 12).

Decorating the apartment can only be carried out with your permission. This includes painting, whacking nails into the walls for pictures and shelves, and so on.

Security needs to be in place if the tenant leaves the property for any length of time. This includes shutting doors and windows and setting the alarm.

The tenant has to pay for any damage to property or utilities.

No pets (unless you don't mind dirty hairs or smells).

Tip

Have a few sets of keys in case they go missing. If you're using a management company, their address should be on the fob, not yours. If you're letting the property yourself, you could use a key-finder company if you don't want people knowing where you live and don't want thieves to fleece the joint. Write the company name and number on the fob; lost keys can then be handed in if they're found. This saves you having to change the locks.

The Lease

It's essential to draw up a detailed lease agreement so that the tenant is clear about the terms of occupancy and rent payments. I can't emphasise enough the need to spell out everything in simple language. Imagine that the tenant is as thick as a plank when you are writing up the agreement. Make everything clear to avoid problems. You can get a lease agreement from the Irish Property Owners Association (IPOA) and you can add to it if you need to. A friend of mine was really sloppy in this area. He didn't define the exact rental terms and didn't record rent payments. The tenant made out that he had paid more rent than he had, and he tried to sue my friend to get the money! The problem was that because the tenant wasn't given a rent book, there was no proof of what had been paid. You should always give a tenant a rent book unless a standing order has been set up for payments, in which case it shows up on a bank statement. Every time rent is paid, you and the tenant should sign for it and date it.

Rent Book

A rent book will contain:

Your name, the address of the property and your contact number

Details of the rent and service charges

The tenancy period

The deposit paid

A furniture inventory

Tenants Can Claim Tax Back

Tenants are entitled to claim VAT back on their rent, so give them your PPS number and receipts for the rent they pay.

Rent Allowance

Under this scheme, the government provides low-income tenants with an allowance towards their rent. If you get a tenant who qualifies for the scheme, the rent is usually (but not always) paid to you directly. You will be asked to fill out a rent-allowance form to verify your details and the amount of rent to be paid.

Security of Tenure

In the past, leases typically spanned a year, but since 2004 a tenant, after a six-month period, has an automatic right to live in a property for four years. For this reason, landlords are reluctant to draw up a lease for any more than six months. If the tenant does happen to stay for more than six months – which gives them the right to stay for four years – the landlord can only end the tenancy for the following reasons:

They want to live in the property themselves.

The property will be sold or refurbished.

The property will be used for another purpose.

The property is not suited to the tenants any more. For example, they may want more people to live in the house than was originally agreed.

The Private Residential Tenancies Board (PRTB)

If you want to let your property, you have to register each tenant with the PRTB within one month of the tenancy. You'll have to fill out a basic form (you can get it online), and it will cost you €70 per tenancy. The board is there to give advice and deal with any problems between landlords and tenants.

Your Relationship with the Tenant

Put simply, be nice but don't become friends. Tenants need to understand that you're their landlord, not someone they can fob off when money's due. Have limited contact with tenants to prevent the whole 'friend' thing developing. Have the rent paid directly into your account via standing order so you don't have to go knocking on doors. Review the rent every year, but if you get good tenants make sure you keep them happy.

Tip

Give your tenants a Christmas present. This could be a bottle of wine, a voucher for somewhere nice or a week's rent free. It doesn't have to be anything major but it keeps them very happy!

Tax on Rental Income

You have to pay income tax on the rent you receive on your property, unless it's within the Rent-a-Room Scheme limit. To keep tax to a minimum, deduct all allowable expenses:

Accountants' fees and mortgage interest payments

Section relief (23 and 50, as explained above)

Refurbishment of the property (contact the local authorities to see if you qualify for the Refurbishment Scheme)

Management and letting fees (advertising, tenancy agreement fees, etc)

Property and mortgage insurance

Service charges

Anything bought for the house, such as furniture and appliances

Security systems

Council Tax

Tip

If you're married, take advantage of personal allowances and lower tax bands. In certain cases, registering the property in one of your names will keep tax down.

9

Selling the Property

'For Sale' signs are popping up all over the place – an indication that people are panicking and want to get out of the property market now that the bubble has burst. And I guess if they took on more than they could chew, they *should* get out. But in a lot of cases, people aren't pulling out of the market due to being financially squeezed. They see everyone else panicking and, without actually thinking about their options, they sell. Trust me, they'll regret it! Unless you're selling either (a) to get out of financial difficulty or (b) to clear the mortgage on your own home, you'd be mad to sell a good property. Interest rates are historically low and we have more payment options available to us now than we ever had. Look at how Ireland is growing. It's expanding by the minute. Although not all the new arrivals will stay in the country in the long term, some of them will. They've set up lives here. As long as there are people living in the country, your property should rent. So think about holding on to your goody rather than selling it; consider fixing the rate to protect yourself from rising rates, and renting it out. If you want to buy more property, and if the deal makes sense, now is not a bad time to buy. Any investor will tell you that to make money from property, you should buy when everyone else is selling.

The question is, then, if I think you shouldn't sell property, why have I bothered including a chapter about it? Well, as I said, I want to give you all the information and help you profit in any way you can. If you decide to sell a property to clear the mortgage on your home, I want you to get the maximum price for it. Clearing the mortgage on a home is the only reason I would sell a property.

Preparing the Property

Selling a property is all about presentation – but the right type of presentation. I'm talking about staging your house for people with no imagination here. A lot of people can't see beyond what a property looks like in its current state, so what happens if your style is fussy and they hate it? To increase your chances of selling a property, you need to play up to a wide audience, so keep things simple, and if potential buyers don't feel like using their imagination, they don't have to. Think about the message you want to give to your target market. Selling property is really about selling a lifestyle. If it's an expensive property, your buyer needs to feel luxurious in it. If your market is a family, the garden and kitchen need to say: 'You can play here.'

The Outside

The property has to be a turn-on from the minute the viewer arrives. First impressions are everything. It's got to say: 'Welcome, I'm your new home and you'll love me.' It should be inviting, free of clutter, clean and well maintained. The lawn should be mowed and the outside of the building should be painted.

Light and Space

Possibly the biggest selling point for any property is light and space. Nobody wants to live in a cave: they want to be able to tell the difference between night and day when they're inside.

Maximise Light

Have a look outside and see if there's anything stopping light getting into the house. Big trees and bushes should be cut back so everything is neat and tidy.

Get your Marigolds out and scrub the windows. You'd be amazed at how much light is blocked by dirt.

Take down mangy net curtains. They look fussy and they block light.

Fit stronger light bulbs than normal when showing buyers around.

Put up a mirror or two to reflect light. Putting the mirror opposite a window really gives the impression of extending an area.

Create Space

Clear away junk. Keep rooms simple and make sure all your ornaments are out of sight, no matter how gorgeous you think they are.

Don't stuff everything into a cupboard if someone will look in it.

Keep furniture to a minimum but don't leave the property empty. An empty room can look just as small as a cluttered room. Keep things simple but not sparse.

Colours should be neutral if possible.

Try not to overdo patterns or wall plates. Scary!

Keep internal doors open. It makes it feel as though one room flows into the next.

Put up blinds rather than curtains and keep them open.

Place a fresh plant in one or two of the rooms. It brings a feeling of the airy outdoors indoors. Fresh flowers do the same. Don't use anything with a strong smell, though.

Make sure the property is well ventilated. Stuffy smells create stuffy feelings. Use a mild air freshener like 'Lily of the Valley'.

The Entrance

The entrance hall is extremely important. If it's dull, cluttered and smelly, buyers won't want to look at the rest of the house. Damp is the worst smell, for sure. The walls should be painted in a light colour, and furniture should be limited to a simple hall table, unless the hall is huge. Place a leafy plant where it looks best.

The Kitchen

The kitchen often clinches the deal, so you have to get it right. It should be squeaky clean. You don't have to have the latest designer kitchen to make it appealing to buyers, either. Just jazz it up a bit.

Replace manky handles and/or doors with modern ones.

Replace rough-looking work surfaces.

Pay attention to the cooker. It's often the first thing people look at when they arrive in the kitchen. If it needs to be replaced, look into getting a trendy second-hand one.

Replace broken tiles. Pop along to a tile shop and there are sure to be some on sale.

Paint dated tiles with neutral-coloured tile paint. Only do this if you can get some good-quality paint at a reasonable price.

Get rid of lino flooring. It's really tacky and cheapens the place straight away. Laminate flooring or simple tiles are a better, inexpensive option for a standard property.

If the kitchen has patio doors, make sure you don't have curtains covering them. Let the buyers see the nice garden, and if it's a warm day, open the doors.

Tip

The kitchen style should suit your market and the property. If the house has the expensive look, a cheap kitchen won't work. The buyers will expect higher standards than in an average property.

The Living Room

This is a room where people want to relax, so it needs to be tidy and comfortable. Keep to a neutral palette to give a peaceful feeling. Pale yellows, browns and beiges work well.

Make sure the fireplace and hearth are clean. If it's winter, put on a fire to create a cosy feeling. If it's cold outside, this'll go down very well.

Play soothing music (classical is best) at a gentle volume. Music influences mood. You want everything to feel calm.

The Bathroom

The taps and toilet should be sparkling. Gone are the student days of brown scum in the toilet and slimy gunk on the sink. No cracked soap allowed for this one. Replace it with a dispenser.

Clean the shower tray well. I once went into a house only to be greeted by a hairy razor, chunks of dead skin and crumbly nails! I nearly puked on the spot. I gag even writing about it.

Don't forget the tiles and grout. I think creepy-crawlies when I see dirty black grout, and buyers will too.

Replace a dodgy toilet seat.

A power shower is a big selling point in high-end properties.

Get rid of an ugly shower curtain and get a new one.

Don't underestimate the power of accessories. You want the buyer to feel that they can pamper themselves in the bathroom. Put shampoo and shower gel in nice bottles, put a group of new candles near the bath (and light them) and display some nice, neatly folded towels.

The bathroom should smell fresh. Put a mild air freshener in it.

The Bedroom

Bedrooms should be simple and restful. Use a few cushions placed neatly on the bed to add a luxury feel.

Make the bed properly and, although this may sound like a no-brainer, open the curtains. I once viewed a place where the bedroom curtains were closed. I presumed someone was asleep and didn't go in. It felt awkward. Never make a potential buyer feel awkward.

Bits and Bobs

Touch up paintwork and woodwork.

Sort out rusty hinges and broken handles on doors. Oil door hinges if they look OK but don't work so well. People will open cupboards.

Stop floorboards from squeaking. Sprinkle with talcum powder so that it goes into the grooves, then vacuum off the rest so that it's clean.

Get rid of cobwebs, especially around light fittings.

Check out any cracks in the ceiling and paint over them.

Make sure carpets are clean and decent. Dirty floors are a real turn-off.

Smells influence emotions. The smells of smoke and pets are possibly the biggest turn-offs. Smells should be fresh and clean. There are smells that are particularly worth paying attention to. These include coffee and freshly baked bread. It's a cliché but it works.

The temperature in the property should be comfortable. If it's too cold or too warm, the viewers won't want to stay to look around.

Keep windows shut if the property is on a busy road to limit the amount of noise.

Clean the window frames.

Getting and Dealing with an Agent

The seller, not the buyer, pays for the estate agent. Property buying and selling is a big business, so competition between agents is high. To get the best price for your property, you will need a good agent, unless you intend selling it yourself. I recommend that you get an agent. They're likely to get a buyer sooner than you would because of their contacts, and if they're good, the sale should go through smoothly. There are plenty of agents around: the real issue is choosing a good one. The agent should tick the following boxes:

They shift properties quickly. You'll know by how often new properties appear in their windows or on their websites.

They have a good reputation, are experienced and can be trusted.

They advertise to the widest possible market. They use various ways of advertising, including broad-based websites like *daft.ie, myhome.ie* and *propertynews.com.*

They have a good high-street location. How easy was it for you to find them?

They can answer questions about the current state of the property market, on both the sales and rental side.

They know the area you're selling in.

They can manage the sale effectively. That includes being able to deal with any problems that may occur during the sale.

They are flexible and accommodating with their time.

They can give you a realistic valuation.

Big developers use them.

Tip

Find out the buyer's circumstances.

Do they have a tight budget, in which case they aren't likely to budge from their offer?

Do they have finance in place, and how quickly could they move with the sale?

Have they any holidays planned or other commitments that might hold up the sale?

Are they flexible with the sale timescale in case your new property isn't ready to move into?

The Valuation

Ask a few agents to visit your property and choose the one you feel most confident in. They'll do what's called a *market appraisal* (a valuation) for you. You will generally have to pay for this, but for some agents it is included in their overall fee. The appraisal is to give you an idea of how much you could expect to get for your property. Don't be afraid to ask them questions.

Tips

Make sure the agent who appraises and talks to you about the property is the agent who will be showing buyers around. They need the right information. When the agent repeatedly says: 'I'll check that out for you'. 'I don't know . . .', it can be annoying, and a sign that they may not be up to the job.

Pay for a decent service. If the agent charges you a pittance, they probably won't be able to afford to market your property to the widest possible audience. Check out what the agent is offering for their fee. Pay for quality service.

The Price

The agent should be able to tell you the right price for your property. It's not your job to come up with the figure, but make sure the valuation the agent gives is realistic. They should also tell you your starting figure, i.e. the price you'd ask for the first few weeks to see if there are any takers.

The Agent's Contract

You'll be asked to sign the agent's contract before they try to sell your property. Like any contract, make sure you read it thoroughly and understand it before signing it. The contract should cover the following:

The fee (including VAT) and when it's payable.

The timeframe on the contract. This should be between six to eight weeks. It'll give the agent
enough time to market the property but is short
enough that you can stop using them if they aren't
able to shift it quickly.

The Viewing

Only allow a potential buyer to view your property in the
company of an agent. Showing someone around yourself
is a bad idea. God knows who the viewer is. Your safety
is paramount. The agent might show them the property
when you're there, but not necessarily. If you want to
pop out for an hour while the viewing takes place, you
can arrange to give the agent the keys. If you do happen
to be there and the agent and buyer arrive, lead them to
the nicest part of the house first and end on a high note
also. First and last impressions have the most impact.
Don't feel the need to entertain. You don't have to rab-
bit on at them, just be welcoming and answer any questions they might have. Questions you might be asked
include:

What are the locals and the area like?

How soon do you want to move?

It's just basic stuff. Leave the rest to the agent. It's
their job to sell the property, not yours.

An Offer

You can never really predict who'll buy your property,
even if a person seems excited during viewing. Sometimes the seemingly lifeless viewers end up buying, so

don't make any judgements during the viewing. Just because someone tells you they love the property doesn't mean anything other than that they are a complimentary person. Wait for the actual offer. If it comes, do one of two things:

Accept the offer from the highest bidder who has finance available and agrees to buy the property within an agreed period of four weeks.

Chance upping the price to see if they bite. If they don't go for it after a few days, let it go for the original price.

If you find that the property isn't selling, you will have to review a few things:

Is the price too high?

Is the agent doing their job right?

What is the state of the property market in general?

Is there anything wrong with the property that might be putting buyers off? If a buyer had a survey done and a problem showed up in the report, it might be worth correcting the problem.

The Survey

The buyer's lender might ask for the property to be surveyed. The buyer usually arranges this through the agent. It is important to beware that if something shows up in the report, it could affect the buyer's offer or their agreement to the sale. We spoke about this earlier from the point of view of your being the buyer.

Tips

If the buyer points out a fault, do the following:

Ask to see the section of the report detailing the fault. If it's legitimate, they shouldn't have a problem showing you.

Ask to see the section of the report showing the surveyor's thoughts on the property and what he thinks it's worth.

Ask for an estimate of the cost of repairing the fault.

Don't risk losing the sale over a few quid. If it's a small reduction, give it.

Sale Agreed

The buyer should put their offer in writing and if the price and conditions suit, you could agree to the sale. Let the agent and your solicitor know, and they'll get things moving.

Memorandum of Sale

I'm sure that the people who coined this term could have come up with a more simple, no-frills expression. This is basically just a letter detailing the people involved in the sale and the price the property will be sold at. The seller, the buyer and each of their solicitors get a copy.

The Agent's Job

The agent's job at this stage is to see that the property sale goes through smoothly. They should:

Ensure the buyer has finance and that it's ready to be issued by the bank. Finance is usually issued after the survey has taken place and the property has been given the OK.

Collect the deposit and the balance of the payment at the appropriate times. This will be in the form of a banker's draft or building society cheque.

Check up on solicitors' progress.

Arrange the survey.

Resolve any delays and other outstanding issues.

Ensure that searches have been carried out and are in order.

Your Solicitor's Job

When they have been notified that the buyer's finances have been arranged and sale proceedings are ready, *they will go ahead with the paperwork.*

They'll draw up the sale contract outlining all the terms and conditions, including a list of any fixtures and fittings agreed in the sale.

They'll ask you to fill out a Property Information Form. This details any alterations made to the property, planning applications accepted or refused, details of boundaries and disputes, and so on. If the property is leasehold, you'll have to give information about the lease.

They'll touch base with the buyer to discuss the sale, read through the contract and sign on the dotted line. All's not done and dusted until the contracts are exchanged, though.

Gazundering

This is where the buyer tries to pull a fast one and reduce their offer a day or two before the sale is completed. This is legal but very annoying. Thankfully, most people aren't this mean, but if it happens, you'll have to make a decision. The question really comes down to this: do you refuse to sell and go back to square one or do you let the property go at the lower price? No doubt the decision would be very tough if you had arranged to move into a new place. I can't tell you what to do on this one, but consider that the buyer may be just chancing their arm. It might not be a bad idea to refuse to budge on price initially. Then, if they won't pay the original agreed price and you don't have another buyer, you might have to bite your tongue and sell.

Exchange of Contracts

This is the point where you and the buyer are legally bound to go through with the sale. The solicitors wrap up everything for you. They'll agree a sale completion date and something called a *requisitions on title* will be sent to your solicitor to say how completion will occur. This will outline things like the method of money transfer and how legal documents and keys will be exchanged.

Tax

Selling a property means giving money to the taxman. You have to pay Capital Gains Tax (CGT): tax on the money gained from the sale. The only time you don't is if you're selling your own home. But remember: unless there's financial difficulty (which there won't be if you do your sums before buying anything) or your portfolio is strong enough to allow you to sell a property to clear debt on your home, think about holding on to a property rather than selling.

The Crew

Make sure you have a good bunch of people around you to help you achieve your goals. The most successful people on the planet always have a good team to support them. The team might include mentors (people who have already achieved your goal, or something similar, and can advise you), your solicitor, your accountant, tradesmen, friends and family. Look at your team as the crew on a ship. The better the crew, the better the journey will be. If you have an incompetent, negative bunch on board, you'll surely sink, but if you have experts, you'll sail free and easy. You'll go places!

Conclusion

It's now time for you to take action. Don't settle for second-best when you don't have to. Rather than seeing obstacles as a problem, see them as a challenge to overcome. Explore all possibilities until you find the ones that work best for you, and then make it happen – even if you think you can't

There are so many things you thought you couldn't do at the time, but despite all odds you achieved them. You learned to walk, you learned to talk and you learned to read – things that, if I asked you to do them now, you'd think were impossible. What's the difference between you learning to do these things as a child and you learning to do them now? Very simple: as a child, you didn't entertain the words 'I can't'. You simply decided what you wanted and took action until you achieved your goal.

As Henry Ford said: 'If you believe you can or if you believe you can't, you're right.' Go to it.

Acknowledgements

My parents, Maureen and Padraig Kennedy, who are and have always been my pillars of strength.

My brothers, sisters, nieces and nephews.

My grandmother and grandfather.

Author Tony Monaghan.

Bill Cullen, John Boyle, Frank Gormley, Tony Robbins, Robert Kyosaki, Pat Slattery (Rainmaker), Brian Colbert, Mark Victor Hansen, Keith Cunningham, Catriona Kelly, Owen Fitzpatrick, Donal O'Leary, Rebecca Morgan and Paul McKenna for inspiring me to live my dreams.

Mary McNamee and Caroline McDonagh for being spectacular.

My amazing friends for bringing sunshine into my life.

The fantastic Powerteam.

Gillian Jordan and Ashling Coyne (the stars in the sky).

Patrick Durcan and Lynda Greenwood.

Grace.

Latitia.